Hernan Cortés and Montezuma: The Conquistador and the Conquered

By Charles River Editors

Moctezuma II in the Codex Mendoza

About Charles River Editors

Charles River Editors was founded by Harvard and MIT alumni to provide superior editing and original writing services, with the expertise to create digital content for publishers across a vast range of subject matter. In addition to providing original digital content for third party publishers, Charles River Editors republishes civilization's greatest literary works, bringing them to a new generation via ebooks.

Visit charlesrivereditors.com for more information.

Introduction

Moctezuma II, from Historia de la conquista de México by Antonio de Solis

Moctezuma II (circa 1466–1520)

"Cortés and all of us captains and soldiers wept for him, and there was no one among us that knew him and had dealings with him who did not mourn him as if he were our father, which was not surprising, since he was so good. It was stated that he had reigned for seventeen years, and was the best king they ever had in Mexico, and that he had personally triumphed in three wars against countries he had subjugated. I have spoken of the sorrow we all felt when we saw that Montezuma was dead. We even blamed the Mercederian friar for not having persuaded him to become a Christian." – Bernal Díaz del Castillo

Nearly 500 years after his death and the demise of his empire, Moctezuma II is the most famous ruler of the most famous civilization in the New World, the Aztec. For centuries the legends surrounding his life and the conquest of the Aztecs by Hernan Cortés have fascinated readers and historians alike.

Moctezuma was born around 1466 in the legendary Aztec city of Tenochtitlán and into the ruling family of the Aztec Confederacy. In the Nahuatl language, his name means "Angry Lord" or "Strong Armed Lord," and he was the ninth ruler of the Aztecs, who called their leaders *tlatoani*. Though he is the best known ruler of the Aztec today, he was actually the second Aztec tlatoani to bear the name Moctezuma, after he assumed the throne from his uncle.

The Spanish conquest of the Aztec and some of the myths and legends surrounding it have made his name (and variations of it like Montezuma) instantly recognizable around the globe, his life is shrouded in mystery; Bernal Diaz del Castillo's *The Conquest of New Spain* and Miguel Leon-Portilla's translation of the Aztec observation of the conquest, *The Broken Spears*, recorded but a few details about the last Aztec ruler's life. Also, these two sources are only concerned with the circumstances surrounding the Spanish conquest of the Aztecs and therefore only deal with the very end of Moctecuma II's life and reign. Thus, his early life largely remains a mystery.

So what is known about the famous Aztec ruler? Naturally, there is still a fierce debate over what happened during the conquest of the Aztec, and one of the most controversial episodes of the conquest was Moctezuma's death. But all of the sources agree that Moctezuma – sometimes called Moctezuma the Younger – generally possessed a reputation as a valiant warrior and was considered a courageous combat leader among his people. Myths and legends have helped fill in the blanks, regardless of their accuracy, and many of them have since become the best known details of Moctezuma's life.

Cortés and Montezuma chronicles the life and legacy of the famous ruler and examines the myths, legends and historical accounts in an attempt to separate fact from fiction. Along with pictures of famous art depicting important people, places, and events, you will learn about Moctezuma II like you never have before.

Hernán Cortés de Monroy y Pizarro (1485-1547)

"Among these temples there is one which far surpasses all the rest, whose grandeur of architectural details no human tongue is able to describe; for within its precincts, surrounded by a lofty wall, there is room enough for a town of five hundred families." – Hernán Cortés

During the Age of Exploration, some of the most famous and infamous individuals were Spain's best known conquistadors. Naturally, as the best known conquistador, Hernán Cortés (1485-1547) is also the most controversial. Like Christopher Columbus before him, Cortés was lionized for his successes for centuries without questioning his tactics or motives, while indigenous views of the man have been overwhelmingly negative for the consequences his conquests had on the Aztecs and other natives in the region. Just about the only thing everyone agrees upon is that Cortés had a profound impact on the history of North America.

Of course, the lionization and demonization of Cortés often take place without fully analyzing the man himself, especially because there are almost no contemporaneous sources that explain what his thinking and motivation was. If anything, Cortés seemed to have been less concerned with posterity or the effects of the Spanish conquest on the natives than he was on relations with the Mother Country itself. Of the few things that are known about Cortés, it appears that he was both extremely ambitious and fully cognizant of politics and political intrigue, even in a New World thousands of miles west of Spain itself. Cortés spent much of his time in Mexico and the New World defending himself against other Spanish officials in the region, as well as trying to portray and position himself in a favorable light back home.

While those ambitions and politics understandably colored his writings about his activities and conquests, scholars nevertheless use what he wrote to gain a better understanding of the indigenous natives he came into contact with. Even then, however, what he wrote was scarce; Cortés's account of his conquest of Mexico is comprised of five letters he addressed to the Holy Roman Emperor, Charles V. As Adolph Francis Bandelier noted in the Catholic Encyclopedia in 1908, "Cortés was a good writer. His letters to the emperor, on the conquest, deserve to be classed among the best Spanish documents of the period. They are, of course, coloured so as to place his own achievements in relief, but, withal, he keeps within bounds and does not exaggerate, except in matters of Indian civilization and the numbers of population as implied by the size of the settlements. Even there he uses comparatives only, judging from outward appearances and from impressions."

Cortés and Montezuma chronicles Cortés's life, but it also examines the aftermath of his conquest and analyzes the controversy surrounding his legacy. Along with pictures of important people, places, and events in his life, you will learn about Cortés like you never have before.

Chapter 1: The Establishment of the Aztec Empire

The man destined to become the Aztec's most famous leader is shrouded in mystery, but to understand him and his empire, it's necessary to understand the history of the Aztec before his reign.

The people group's name *Aztec* refers to their northern homeland, Aztlan, but the Aztecs did not refer to themselves as Aztecs. Some have implied that Aztlan refers to an area in the Southwestern United States occupied by the "Pueblo peoples" and characterized by archaeological sites like Chaco Canyon and various Pueblo peoples' sites located in and around the "four corners" formed by the intersection of the borders of the present-day states of Colorado, Utah, New Mexico, and Arizona. This area was heavily impacted by a widespread and possibly global drought that occurred after 1150 A.D. that coincided with the collapse of the Pueblo cultures as well as those of the Mississippian Cultures (The Mound Builders) and the Tiwanaku culture around Lake Titicaca in present-day highland Bolivia. Given the complete collapse of society that would accompany such a multi-year drought and the continental effect of this series of droughts, it is conceivable that the Aztecs were indeed indigenous to the present-day Southwestern United States and wandered southward and into present-day Mexico in search of more hospitable environs.

According to the Aztecs' foundational history, which was almost certainly revised (inaccurately) by Moctezuma's great-grandfather Moctezuma I, the group traveled from their ancestral homeland called Aztlan, and while on this journey, which lasted for some 200 years, the Aztecs wandered throughout Northern Mexico, eventually entering the Valley of Mexico around 1248. By the time the they arrived in the Valley of Mexico, it was completely occupied by a number of city-states. The city-states in the valley were Chalco, Xochimilco, Tlacopan, Atzcapotzalco, and Culhuacan among others. Of these city-states, the most powerful were Culhuacan on the south shore of Lake Texcoco and Atzcapotzalco on the western shore were the most powerful. Lake Texcoco occupied much of the valley and was a rare water source for the peoples who settled there. The nomadic Mexica first tried to settle on a hill called Chapultepec (the hill of grasshoppers) on the western shore of Lake Texcoco and were soon ousted from there by the Tepanecs of Atzcapotzalco, but Cocoxtli–the tlatoani of Culhuacan–allowed them to settle in an unoccupied area called Tizaapan around 1299. After settling there, they were also absorbed into the Culhuacan culture and intermarried with them.

About twenty-five years later (in 1323 AD), the Aztec approached Achicometl, the new tlatoani of Culhuacan, asking if they could have his daughter to render her into the goddess Yaocihuatl. Presuming that the relative newcomers to the Valley of Mexico intended to honor his daughter, the unwitting ruler agreed, and his daughter was sacrificed, thus joining the Aztec pantheon of gods and goddesses. According to legend, Achicometl was invited to an honorific dinner at which a priest, wearing the princess's flayed skin, with her hands and feet still attached, emerged and performed a ritual dance. The ruler and his people were understandably incensed and immediately forced them out of the area. The fleeing Aztecs, responding to a prophecy from their god Huitzilopochtli which stated that they should settle when they saw the sign of an eagle sitting upon a cactus with a snake in its talons, settled on a marshy island off of the western shore of Lake Texcoco. There they began to build what would eventually become their capital, Tenochtitlán. *Tenocha*, being one name the Aztecs used to describe themselves, and the suffix *titlan*, which in Nahuatl means *the place of*. So, simply put, Tenochtitlán refers to the place of the Tenocha. Using *chinampas* (floating pallets, loaded with lake-bed soil and planted with crops) the small island grew quite large; the plants growing on the chinampas would eventually grow through the pallet and anchor themselves in the lake bottom, anchoring the chinampa and slowly increasing the size of the island. A second group settled on the north side of the island and founded the city of Tlatelolco. Originally founded as an independent city, it would eventually be absorbed by Tenochtitlán and would become a "quarter" of the sprawling Aztec capital.

The growing Aztec city-state, having adopted the customs of Culhuacan, elected its first Tlatoani in 1376. For roughly the next fifty years, the Aztecs hired themselves out as mercenaries and their first few tlatoanis were vassals of Atzcapotzalco's leaders. Some time around 1426, the death of their leader caused unrest and eventually a civil war for succession among the Tepanecs of Atzcapotzalco. The Aztecs backed a Tepanec ruler whose reign was cut short, by his brother who usurped the throne and then turned upon those who had allied against him. Despite the death of their tlatoani, Chimalpopoca, the Aztecs remained defiant. The leader of Texcoco fled and recruited allies from the tlatoani of Huexotzinco (a nearby city-state), and the Aztecs allied themselves with Tlacopan a Tepanec vassal city-state in rebellion against Atzcapotzalco. Through this alliance and the defeat of Atzcapotzalco, the Aztecs became an independent city-state and established a colony on the shore of Lake Texcoco. Around 1428, Tenochtitlán entered into the Triple Alliance with the city-states of Texcoco and Tlacopan, and until the arrival of Cortes and the Spanish in 1520 this alliance systematically built a massive confederacy, demanding and receiving tribute from the surrounding city-states. Gradually, as Tlacopan and Texcoco faded from power, Tenochtitlán and the Aztecs assumed sole control of the wide-ranging confederacy.

The Aztecs' governmental organization is often described as an "empire", but this is an inaccurate description. Rather, the territory the Aztecs controlled functioned more like a vast confederacy, extending from the Gulf of Mexico and to the Pacific Ocean. The Aztec tlatoanis built the confederacy by invading regions and threatening to release their army. The subjugated rulers remained in control of their city-states, but the Aztecs forced them to agree to certain caveats. First, the subjugated peoples would provide sacrificial victims, usually female virgins, though male warriors were also acceptable and sometimes preferred. Second, the absorbed city-state would accept and agree to worship the Aztecs' gods, while the Aztecs agreed to do the same for the gods of the subjugated city-state. Third, the vassal city-states would provide tribute to the Aztecs in the form of gold and other items valued by the Aztecs (quetzal feathers, cacao beans etc.). These stipulations were usually easily met because the Aztec army had a reputation for extreme brutality and was easily the most powerful military organization in the area.

Chapter 2: The Coronation of Moctezuma II

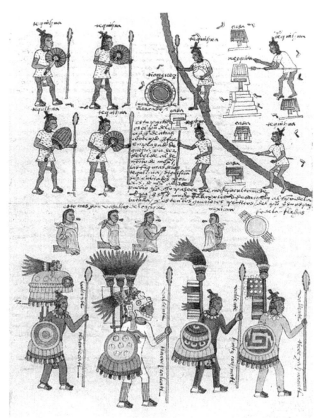

From the Codex Mendoza: (top) Warriors scout a town at night in preparation for an attack. (middle) Negotiations after surrender. (bottom) High-ranking commanders.

In 1426, the royal palace elite of Tenochtitlán elevated the war lord Itzacóatl (native for obsidian serpent) to the throne, and he chose as his second in command, Cihuacoatl (snake woman). Together they set about consolidating their empire by subduing the cities around the lake, which were then required to render tribute to the Aztec king. He was succeeded by

Moctezuma I (or Montezuma I), who ruled from 1440-1468. Along with his younger brother Tlacaélel, they expanded the Aztec tributary region, and the Aztec empire was further consolidated and expanded by Ahuitzotl, who assumed power in 1486. According to primary sources, Moctezuma II ascended to the throne in 1503.

Like his predecessors, Moctezuma was expected to add to the Aztecs' territory since his ascension to the throne as *Huey-tlatoani* (meaning Honored or Elder Speaker), as the Aztecs had come to name their rulers. Moctezuma assumed the throne after a multi-day ceremony and festival, which culminated on July 15, 1503, recorded on his coronation stone as the Aztec calendar day 11 Crocodile, 1 Reed. Like many cultures all over the globe, the Aztecs collected and embraced practices and technologies from the peoples they encountered. Their calendar is an example of one of these technologies that many Mesoamerican peoples used, probably adopted from the Maya city-states, located throughout present-day Central and Southern Mexico, Guatemala, Belize, and Honduras. The calendar itself is a composed of two cycles, one of 260 days and one of 360 days. The cycles themselves are composed of either thirteen or eighteen months of twenty days each. The 360-day cycle also had five feast or holy days added to it for a total of 365.

Aztec feather headdress attributed to Moctezuma II exhibited at the Museo Nacional de Antropología e Historia, México.

After being named the next Huey-tlatoani, but prior to ascending to the throne, Moctezuma engaged in a series of "coronation wars." The purpose of these wars was to secure sacrificial victims that would be used in Moctezuma's coronation rituals and to again prove the new tlatoani's prowess in battle. After the days-long rituals that sealed Moctezuma's assumption of the Aztec throne, he would don a triangular, turquoise crown that marked the Aztecs' Huey-tlatoani and ordered the construction of a massive new palace.

Unfortunately, most of the buildings and other potential archaeological evidence surrounding Moctezuma's rule has been lost, but some sculptures and other fragments have been excavated from the palace site, located beneath the Palacio Nacionál in central Mexico City. Among the salvaged sculptures is the Huey-tlatoani's coronation stone, which remains relatively undamaged. The coronation stone bears Aztec iconography and the official date of Moctezuma's assumption of the throne.

Much of the iconography used by the Aztecs and their rulers referred to Tula, a city-state that had risen and collapsed prior to the ascendancy of the Aztec. Also, present are references to the god Quetzalcoatl (the Feathered Serpent) and symbols that demonstrate the Huey-tlatoani's control of wealth and sustenance–often ears of corn. The Huey-tlatoani's image was tightly controlled, and he was always presented to his people as a semi-divine being. One sculpture depicts a seated Moctezuma performing the ritual auto-sacrificial blood-letting. Opposite him is Quetzalcoatl, performing the same ritual, meant to establish Moctezuma as an equal with the deity. In another sculpture, Moctezuma is shown standing on one side of the solar disk (The Aztec Calendar) while on the other side is Huitzilopochtli (the Mexica's tribal god). Both figures are shown holding the maguey spines used in ritual bloodletting; Moctezuma's depiction here shows him as a primary actor in the progress of the universe. As was typical of leaders throughout Mesoamerica – and much of the ancient world – Aztec tlatoanis were often associated with deities to establish and/or reaffirm their right to reign.

Aztec Ritual Sacrifice, Codex Tudela, 16th century based on an earlier work. Museo de América, Madrid

For the roughly twenty years that Moctezuma reigned over the Aztecs as Huey-tlatoani, he systematically increased the size of the territory the Aztec controlled, as had the tlatoani before him. When the Spaniards landed on the Gulf of Mexico coast near present-day Veracruz, Veracruz, Mexico, the Aztecs' confederacy had reached its zenith.

Chapter 3: Cortés' Early Years

Hernán Cortés was born on an uncertain date in 1485 in Medellín, in the Spanish province of Extremadura. A dry, dusty, and hot backwater in the southwest of Spain, Extremadura was the home of many families of noble descent who had fallen into poverty, and it would prove to be the breeding ground of a majority of the conquistadors, most of whom came from honorable lineages but had few viable prospects in their native country. Indeed, this was the case for Hernán, son of Martín Cortés de Monroy and Catalina Pizarro Altamarino (through his mother,

Cortés was a distant cousin of the conqueror of Peru, Francisco Pizarro). Though he is commonly referred to as Hernán today, he called himself Hernando or Fernando during his life.

The Spanish nobility was traditionally a warrior caste forged in the *reconquista*, the slow but ultimately successful reincorporation of the Iberian peninsula into Christendom at the expense of the Arabic-speaking Muslims who had ruled it for centuries. Cortés's father, a captain in the military, had remained true to the martial vocation of his class, but it held little tangible reward now that the Moors had been finally driven back into North Africa in 1492, the same year that Christopher Columbus first arrived in the New World thinking it was Asia.

At the time of Cortés's birth, "Spain" as a cohesive entity did not exist. Rather, the Iberian Peninsula was composed of numerous small principalities, each ruled by a monarch. By the time of Cortés's birth, these monarchs, working in concert, were engaged in the final years of a campaign to oust the Moors, who had been occupying the bulk of the Iberian Peninsula since 711. Over the course of nearly eight centuries, the Spanish gradually pushed the Moorish forces south, eventually defeating them finally at the Battle of Granada in 1491. On January 2, 1492, King Ferdinand II of Aragon and Queen Isabella I of Castile assumed control of Granada. About 9 months later, Columbus landed in the New World.

The significance of The Battle of Granada and 1492 was the fact that it freed military and financial resources from the burden of liberating the peninsula from its Moorish occupiers. The age of exploration that ensued and Portugal and Spain's early dominance in that exploration is largely a product of both the elimination of the need for internal military operations and the development of superior military technology. Additionally, the large numbers of highly proficient military forces and leaders were easily adapted to the coming Spanish exploration and expansion. The conquistadors who would conquer the Americas in the name of Iberian monarchs were direct products of centuries of military conflict on the Iberian Peninsula.

Apparently a bright and ambitious child, Hernán Cortés left home for the prestigious University of Salamanca at the age of 14 with the intention of studying law. His parents, like many today, probably saw the legal profession as a steady and promising career path for their son, one which might help him restore the family's diminished fortune. But Cortés only remained at the university for two years, thus falling short of earning a degree. His evident impatience with the need for prolonged, sustained study reveals the restlessness and impetuousness that would become one of his most prevalent character traits. On the other hand, his legal studies provided him with knowledge that would later prove valuable when he was attempting to justify his claims to the land he conquered across the ocean and negotiate with the Spanish crown over his share of its wealth.

Thus, two of the qualities that Cortés would share with later conquistadors are evident from his early choices. First, he did not wish to follow a slow, gradual route to wealth and prominence; he wanted to achieve these things in a dramatic and immediate fashion. Second, he was willing to use the most influential forms of knowledge of the time and place, especially law and theology, to pursue his own aims, but he had no real reverence for learning in itself. His departure from Salamanca set a pattern. As he would do again and again, he left behind the old, the familiar, and established for the new, the uncertain, and the adventurous.

Spain's great writer Miguel de Cervantes, in a story about a man from Extremadura, described the Americas as "the refuge of the despairing sons of Spain, the church of the homeless, the asylum of homicides, the haven of gamblers and cheats, the general receptacle for loose women, the common center of attraction for many, but effectual resource of very few." As a contemporary view of the conquistadors and other arrivistes in the new colonies, Cervantes's is not a flattering portrait of what motivated men like Cortés to make the dangerous crossing of the Atlantic. And yet from what we know of his personality and early life, it seems like an accurate enough characterization of the man and the circles he frequented. A restless, mischievous young man, he found employment as a notary in the port city of Seville, but he soon found himself attracted to the new lands to the West, for which ships were departing regularly from Seville's harbor, and from which new wealth was arriving and remaking the city's economy.

When he departed for the island of Hispaniola in 1504, the memory of Columbus's discoveries was still fresh in the minds of the Spanish public. Columbus himself was still alive, but as a result of his disastrous stint as governor of Hispaniola, he had been relieved of his title of Viceroy of the Indies, and the crown had moved to centralize control over the new colonies and ensure their profitability. And though Columbus's voyage to the New World is remembered as one of the seminal events of the last millennium, at the time it still represented a bit of a disappointment. After all, Columbus's goal had been to reach Asia and ensure Spain's access to the trade in luxurious commodities such as spices and silk, and he had also hoped, later in his career, to reach the legendary gold mines of King Solomon.

Instead, what he had actually achieved was now uncertain, but it was becoming clear that rather than reaching the eastern edge of Asia, Columbus had arrived at a different land mass altogether. Justifying himself by the claim that the natives were barbaric heathens who needed to be civilized and converted to Christianity, Columbus had initiated a treatment of the native inhabitants that was at best paternalistic and at worst horrifically brutal and exploitative.

Making matters worse, Columbus had attempted to exploit the islands of Hispaniola and Cuba for gold only to find that the deposits were scarce. In the meantime, a system of thinly disguised slave labor came into being under the name of the *encomienda*, or "entrustment." The notion was that Spanish settlers would be granted a piece of land and power over the natives who inhabited it; their responsibility would be to instruct the natives in religion, in return for which "service" they could exact tributes of gold or other valuables, or labor in extractive or agricultural activities. The system laid the ground for the plantation-slave economy that would later become prevalent in the Caribbean.

It was into this environment that Cortés arrived in 1504, still not yet 20. Although Columbus had met with a friendly reception from the inhabitants of the islands he first visited, the conflict between Spanish settlers and natives had now become implacable. Understandably, the natives were not fond of the *encomienda* system or of the extreme savagery and cruelty of many Spaniards, and some had taken up arms against the new arrivals. One of Cortés's first experiences in the New World was to participate in expeditions against the remaining groups of Indians who had not yet been subjugated. It was here that he got his first taste of the casual brutality of the colonial frontier culture, as well as of the rewards that military exploits could bring. Through his military involvement, Cortés was granted a large *encomienda* in Hispaniola, including control over several hundred subjugated natives. In the meantime, he also offered his services as a notary and clerk to other settlers, establishing a fruitful set of relationships with the colonial authorities.

Just over five years after arriving in the Indies, Cortés would move on from Hispaniola and take part in an expedition to Cuba, a larger island with far more as yet unconquered land. In 1511, Cortés accompanied Diego Velázquez de Cuellar on that expedition, and by 1515 the Spanish colony at Havana had been founded and would serve as a staging point for Spanish forays onto the North American mainland. Bernal Diaz del Castillo describes Spanish efforts at colonizing Mesoamerica in present-day Mexico. While Diaz del Castillo offers a very detailed description of the events, his history makes every effort to present the actions of the Spaniards as pure and honorable (or at least as honorable as military conquest can be), and the author always minimizes the guilt of the conquistadors during the conquest. As an example, he describes in detail how the Spaniards make preparations for all-out war and advance into Tabascan territory, only to blame the Native American for unwarranted attacks against the European invaders. Diaz del Castillo also expends considerable energy refuting an alternate account of the Cortés expedition written by Francisco Lopez de Gomara, who had never been to the Americas but interviewed Cortés and other members of his expedition after the fact. De Gomara also drew criticism from other members of the Cortés expedition for inaccuracies presented in his narrative.

Diaz del Castillo's history also describes the Spaniards' often-bloody interactions with Maya city-states in the present-day Yucatán peninsula during expeditions conducted prior to the Cortés expedition. Juan de Grijalva had explored the eastern coast of Mexico during an expedition in 1518, and this inspired the Spanish to attempt to colonize the Mexican mainland. Cortés's services to the new governor of Cuba, Diego Velázquez, earned him a prominent position in the new colony and helped set about the conditions that made him the one who would lead an expedition to the mainland. He became clerk and secretary to the governor himself, gained control of a large *encomienda*, and accumulated enough prestige to become mayor of the city of

Santiago. However, he soon got ahead of himself, amassing debts through an extravagant lifestyle and gaining the hostility of the governor on account of his unapologetic ambition and his seduction of the governor's sister-in-law, Catalina Juárez, whom Cortés ultimately married. Furthermore, he proved not to be a model citizen of the colony.

According to chronicler Bernal Díaz del Castillo, who would accompany Cortés on his expedition to Mexico, the soon-to-be conquistador was a dandy, a lover of fineries, and unrestrained spender; despite his apparent wealth, Cortés accumulated vast debts during his years in Cuba through his luxurious lifestyle. Such a predicament provides a relatively banal explanation for his desire to set off and conquer new lands. If he was ever going to repay his creditors, he would need a windfall much bigger than the *encomienda* he had already acquired. By obtaining the title of Captain General, necessary for leading further expeditions, Cortés also obtained a higher credit limit, so to speak, because his creditors would now be guaranteed a share of any further profits he obtained.

Chapter 4: Cortés Heads to the Mainland

Once he had gained his commission in 1518, Cortés wasted no time in gathering a fleet of ships and an army of ambitious followers, to whom he promised riches and land. In addition to permanently defraying his debts, Cortés now aimed to establish a permanent presence on the *terra firma*, which no Spaniard had yet accomplished since Columbus's failed attempt to colonize what is now Panama nearly 20 years earlier.

The following year, Cortés, then aged thirty-four, was given command of a flotilla of ten ships and roughly 300 men and charged with sailing to the coast of Mexico and establishing trade with the indigenous people there. Initially, Velázquez, who had been appointed the Governor of Cuba, supported Cortés's expedition, but because of his personal enmity for Cortés, he changed his mind and ordered Cortés to disband his flotilla and expeditionary force just prior to the scheduled launch. Velázquez apparently had an inkling of the fame and wealth that Cortés would achieve if he did manage to colonize the mainland and certainly did not trust Cortés to follow the orders he was given.

When the fleet was nearly organized and ready to depart, the governor attempted twice to intervene and relieve Cortés of his leadership. Velázquez first sent a messenger whom Cortés promptly ordered killed, showing perhaps for the first time the full extent of his ruthlessness, and by the time Velázquez intervened a second time, Cortés was already just about to set sail and simply departed in direct defiance of his superior. Thus, when his 11 ships departed with a crew of over 500 men, they did so in open mutiny, taking advantage of the automatic delay that would be required for the governor to gather another expedition to go after them. Given that Cortés had invested a great deal of his personal wealth and gone into considerable debt to finance his excursion, it is not entirely surprising that he would behave with this degree of audacity. He likely sensed that he had lost the good will of Velázquez and would not be given another opportunity after this. Had he remained, he would have been at the mercy of his creditors and without any obvious way of turning his situation around, since he had already risen about as high as he was likely to in Cuba. His future was by no means guaranteed at this point, but he could be sure that he had few other options than to stake everything on success.

Thus, on February 10, 1519, the fleet of eleven ships departed individually from Cuba with orders to follow the Mexican coast to the island of Cozumel. Sailing from the southeastern end of the island of Cuba in early 1519, the closest stretch of coast Cortés and his crew would find on the mainland was the Yucatán peninsula, once home to the large and wealthy Mayan empire. The Maya had in recent centuries fragmented into smaller sub-groups and city states, and their wealth was now diminished. Previous Spaniards had found little success in the region, and Cortés probably set his sights somewhere else even before he landed, but he did spend some time on the island of Cozumel, just off the Yucatán coast. Although he did not send a large land expedition into the peninsula, he acquired some of his most valuable assets there. First, he came across a Spaniard, survivor of a 1511 shipwreck, who had been living among the Mayas ever since. This man, Gerónimo de Aguilar, was now fluent in the Yucatec Mayan language, but he was also eager to return to his own people. Cortés took Aguilar in, and with that he had something that earlier conquistadors had lacked: a fully bilingual translator.

Aguilar's language skills, though, would have been of little use among the Nahuatl-speaking peoples further to the west had it not been for a second key encounter. On the other side of the Yucatán peninsula, Cortés was given possession of a young woman by the chief of another group of Mayas. This woman, it turned out, was a native of central Mexico and a fluent speaker of Nahuatl, as well as of Mayan and other languages. Cortés called her Doña Marina, but her original name was probably Malinalli, and she would later become known as Malintzin or Malinche to Mexicans. With the combined services of Aguilar and Doña Marina, Cortés now had the ability to communicate fluently with most of the peoples of Mexico, a capacity that gave him a crucial advantage in information gathering over earlier explorers such as Columbus, who proceeded with at-best rudimentary translation services, even in his later travels. Through the communicative chain he was able to establish, Cortés was able to find out not only the location of the great and wealthy Aztec empire, but also the resentment many neighboring tribes felt towards the Aztecs, a hostility he would make use of for his own purposes.

By the time he had made his way past the Yucatecan coast, Cortés seemed to know he wanted to reach what is to this day the Mexican heartland, the central valley of Mexico surrounding the city of Tenochtitlán. He had learned from many sources by now that this was the center of the region's most powerful and wealthy empire. If the reports proved true, Cortés knew, he would be able to accomplish something that had eluded previous Spanish explorers. When Columbus had set out in 1492, his goal was to establish contact with the great urban empires of Asia, places of immense wealth and sophistication. Instead, he had found a series of islands populated by people who were remarkable poor and simple by European standards. They did not live in cities or practice large-scale commerce or even possess more than small quantities of gold. If the Aztecs proved as wealthy as he had been told, Cortés would succeed where Columbus had failed. Within this context, his continued defiance of the orders of the colonial authorities makes sense: a conquest of the scale he was envisioning would so impress the Spanish crown that both his infractions and his debts would be instantly forgiven.

Before Cortés proceeded, he had to ensure that he would have no further trouble from his superiors in Cuba. To achieve the autonomy he sought, he took two major steps. First, upon arriving to the stretch of the Gulf Coast nearest to the Aztec heartland, he established the city of Veracruz, complete with a mayor and city council drawn from among his men. By way of this legal slight of hand, Cortés could claim that he no longer needed to report to the governor of Cuba, since the legitimate authorities of an independent city reported directly to Charles V, the King of Spain. Second, Cortés took the dramatic step of burning his ships in the harbor, signaling that he and his men would not be returning any time soon. Once again, the action suggests a remarkable impetuousness and willingness to gamble for high stakes. It was by no means certain that the ploy to elude Velázquez's authority would actually work, since it was possible that the Spanish crown would refuse to acknowledge Cortés's new settlement, but it would take months for news of Cortés's actions to reach Spain, and it would be several more before orders returned to Cortés himself.

In the meantime, Cortés began to establish contact both with local tribes, some of whom expressed to him their frustration with Aztec rule, and with emissaries of Moctezuma II. The Spaniards bided their time on the coast for some weeks, exchanging messages with the Aztecs and attempting to glean more information before proceeding, since they still had little sense of the exact scale of the kingdom they were planning to take on. When Moctezuma became aware of the strangers in his territory, he responded in a mainly friendly and hospitable manner, repeatedly sending them gifts and inviting them to remain on the land if they were willing to move their settlement somewhat further away from the capital. Not surprisingly, the Spaniards refused that offer.

Cortés's reaction as described in *The Broken Spears*, wondering whether the small, gold trinkets were the only gifts the Aztecs would use to greet visitors, seems a more accurate description of the conquistadors' goals than that of Diaz del Castillo, who constantly down-plays the Spanish hunger for gold. This assessment is based on their later behavior while in Tenochtitlán. Also, it should be understood that news of the arrival of the marauding strangers had already reached Tenochtitlán, and Moctezuma had sent these messengers to determine who the strangers were. The Huey-tlatoani was likely uncertain whether the Spaniards were accompanying the returning Quetzalcoatl, and his uncertainty contributed to the outcome of the conquest. Though often depicted as waffling and indecisive, Moctezuma merely wanted to ensure he did not insult the returning god and thus incur his wrath. The aftermath of the initial contact between the Aztec messengers and the conquistadors also differs greatly between the two texts.

Diaz del Castillo writes that the messengers were given gifts and happily returned to their homes. In *The Broken Spears*, the indigenous writers record that Cortés commended the Aztecs on their prowess in battle but insists that he must see their courage to believe it. He issued the messengers spears and swords and informs that the following morning they will face the Spaniards in single combat, so Cortés could assess their fighting skill. The Aztecs were then allowed to leave, and they paddled furiously away from the Spanish ships and after landing on shore, hurried inland. They did not stop until they were well away from the coast and safe from the conquistadors. The messengers paused to take a meal and were encouraged to stop and rest for a day by the tlatoani of Cuetlaxtlan, where they had rested while journeying to the coast. Citing their obligation to the Huey-tlatoani, they refused the offer and rushed back to Tenochtitlán to inform Moctezuma of their findings. The group entered the Aztec capital during the night, having traveled virtually non-stop.

The following morning, Good Friday, 1519, Cortés and his men went ashore. After ordering his artillery to assume a position atop some nearby sand dunes, the party began building shelters for the men and horses. This work lasted throughout the day, and on Saturday, a group of Native Americans, sent by Quitlalpitoc, the Aztec appointed governor of the region. The Aztec representatives brought gifts of gold trinkets and food and assisted the Spaniards in completing their shelters. They also reported that Quitlalpitoc would visit the Spanish the next day. On Easter Sunday, 1519, Quitlalpitoc and another governor, Teuthlille, arrived and greeted the conquistadors again bearing gifts of gold and foodstuffs. Cortés immediately began pressing the Aztec representatives to bring him to Moctezuma's court, but they delayed and were reluctant to do so, likely following orders from their Huey-tlatoani.

These greetings and arrivals continued for roughly ten days, as the conquistadors received gifts of gold and food–a massive, gold solar disk (commonly referred to as the Aztec calendar) and a lunar disk of silver–that they returned with worthless gifts of colored glass beads and other small gifts. Throughout these visits, Cortés pressed the Aztecs' messengers and governors to escort him to Moctezuma's court, always claiming that he wished to show his obeisance to the Huey-tlatoani, but showing their shrewd judgment of the conquistador's character, they consistently refused, always asking that the Spaniard wait for one reason or another. The frequency of the visits gradually diminished until one morning the Spaniards awoke to find themselves alone and their small settlement abandoned by the Aztecs' vassals. By this point, the conquistadors had become dependent upon the indigenous gifts of food and were soon starving and very short of food. About this time, the Spaniards began grumbling and arguing among themselves, many (especially those allied to Velázquez) voicing a desire to return to Cuba, saying they had gathered sufficient gold and were now starving. This fact, relayed by Diaz del Castillo, also demonstrates the Spaniards' true and primary goal of finding gold, and it illustrates but one of the contradictions within the conquistador's narrative that become clear and evident to anyone who reads his account. On the one hand, he states the Spaniards' only goals were to meet the indigenous people, spread Christianity, and establish trade, while on the other, he repeatedly comments on both how the Spaniards traded for gold–constantly insinuating that the indigenous people did not truly value the precious metal–and commenting on the relative low quality of the gold they acquired.

The Spaniards were eventually forced to advance inland and soon encountered a Totonac city-state, where they made allies of the leaders. After the now-common exchange of gold (on the parts of the indigenous people) for valueless glass beads and other trinkets, Cortés promised his friendship to the Totonac caciques. During one meeting with the Totonac leaders, a party of five Aztec "tax-collectors" arrived in the town, seeking to collect a tax composed of sacrificial victims. Seeing the opportunity to once again fool the indigenous people, Cortés ordered the "tax collectors" seized and bound on a rod with a rope around their necks–as they would bind sacrificial victims. All the while, the conquistador also ensured that no one mentioned his complicity in the seizure of the Aztec representatives. Later that evening, Cortés had the prisoners brought to him secretly and while feigning his ignorance, asked why they had been bound. Cortés told the "tax collectors" that he would free them and hoped that they would return to Moctezuma and report his kindness and his desire to honor and serve the Huey-tlatoani. Through this and other deceptions and lies, Cortés managed to turn some of the vassal states of the Aztecs against their rulers and was eventually able to raise an army of some 2,000 warriors from one city-state (Sempoalla) to attack another city-state (Tzinpantzinco), under the auspices of liberating the latter from the occupation of an Aztec military column that had been dispatched to the town to free the previously imprisoned "tax collectors." The Aztec column, finding no imprisoned tax collectors, had retreated, but Cortés utilized the alternating fear of his force and fear of the Aztecs to further deceive the caciques of Tzinpantzinco, and again managed to lie his way through recruiting more indigenous troops to his cause. Ironically, Diaz del Castillo describes all of Cortés calculated lies as examples of the commander's "justice," while the attempts by the indigenous leaders to appease the invaders *and* their Aztec masters are described as a "pack of lies." By this observation, one can begin to understand the utter fear inspired by the Aztecs' rule, and the complete hypocrisy of the Spaniards is made evident when Diaz del Castillo describes how the caciques of Sempoalla and Tzinpantzinco offered their daughters to the Spaniards. The conquistadors, led by Cortés, "joyfully accepted of the young women" but demanded that the women be converted to Catholicism (baptized) and the caciques end their indigenous religious practices, especially human sacrifices. The caciques were greatly angered by the request that they stop their religious practices and determined to defend their temples. Upon hearing this, Cortés ordered his men to prepare for war–in clear view of the caciques and their warriors–and reminded the caciques of the possible imminent arrival of an Aztec army. Caught between the Spaniards and the Mexica, the caciques chose to submit to the conquistadors and allowed the destruction of their temples and their idols. However, when about fifty Spaniards began tearing down the statues and altars the warriors began to threaten to attack. In response, Cortés had the caciques seized and told them that they would be killed if they did not order their men to stop their attack; the Totonac leaders immediately complied.

At this point, Cortés sent one ship, bearing gold and other gifts directly to Spain. According to Diaz del Castillo, after the departure of the ship bound for Spain, the men voted on two measures. The first elected Cortés their Captain-General and the second mandated that they destroy their remaining ships by running them ashore. Before grounding the ships, the conquistadors removed everything that might serve them during their coming campaign including sails, anchors, ropes, and the ships' boats. In destroying the ships, Cortés's hoped to eliminate the possibility for further mutiny by Velázquez's agents. Additionally, Cortés's previous deceptions had convinced a number of the caciques of the settlements around present-day Veracruz to rebel against Moctezuma. After this, Cortés and his men began to prepare for the march to Tenochtitlán.

Historians have long speculated over why Moctezuma was so generous and seemingly unsuspicious toward the invaders who would soon bring about his demise. The most popular claim is that the arrival of Cortés and his men coincided with a long-prophesied return of the god Quetzalcoatl, said to be a light-haired and light-skinned being who would arrive from across the sea; Moctezuma's deference, in this account, would be the result of his fear that he was dealing with a god rather than a man. However, more recent analysis has suggested that the Quetzalcoatl legend was developed after the conquest, specifically as a way for the Aztec elite to explain the sudden and traumatic liquidation of their entire world. A more reasonable explanation may be based on local politics: Moctezuma knew that his rule was vulnerable and that he had many rivals in and out of Tenochtitlán, so he may have hoped to keep the strangers loyal to him lest they provide aid to his enemies.

If that was the case, Moctezuma actually proved quite prescient, because this is exactly the approach Cortés adopted. He made contact with several of the tribes that deeply resented Aztec rule and promised to support them in a war against their oppressors. What Moctezuma did not seem prepared for, though, was Cortés's endless capacity for treachery and duplicity. He remained in apparently friendly contact with Moctezuma for weeks, accepting gifts and sending more in exchange, even as he was steadily building up an army of indigenous allies who would help him take on the Aztecs. All evidence suggests that Moctezuma was a deeply honorable ruler who remained committed to basic rules and principles of decency and hospitality, and to his detriment he seemed to assume that these new arrivals would behave similarly. But Cortés, as his interactions with Velázquez have already demonstrated, had little use for deference to authority and did not consider customs worth much. His cynical act of establishing a city in order to circumvent the governor's authority suggests Cortés saw rules and laws as things to be manipulated in order to pursue his goals. He took the same approach in his interactions with the Aztec ruler.

Religion provided another fruitful area for Cortés's manipulations. While still on the Gulf Coast, he began attempting to evangelize the native inhabitants – essentially demanding that they accept Christianity or face the consequences. Given what is known of his unscrupulous character, it is difficult to imagine that the conquistador earnestly wished to bring these people to the true faith. But religion proved useful to him in several ways. For one, it allowed him to sanctify a mission that otherwise seemed transparently motivated by greed and egotism. This would prove particularly helpful in gaining royal support back in Spain, since the most widely accepted justification for conquests was that they were a way of spreading the faith. After all, this principle was at the basis of the *encomienda* system, since the holder of an encomienda was charged with instructing his subordinates in religion. Second, the natives understood from their own belief system that to accept a conqueror's rule also included accepting the conqueror's god. When Cortés and his men destroyed the native idols in a temple and replaced them with crucifixes and virgins, it was above all a gesture of power. Third, and even more cynically, religion provided a pretext for unleashing violence. When natives refused to accept the gospel and persisted in their allegedly satanic practices, Cortés used this recalcitrance as a justification for attacking and killing them, since rejection of Christ could be presented as an act of aggression equivalent to war. Several of the most brutal massacres against unarmed people he and his men carried out were performed in the midst of rituals, so that they could claim that they had used force to prevent their victims from carrying out their pagan rites. Cortés was adept at rhetorical displays of piety, but his behavior in war was so craven and so blatantly un-Christian that many contemporaries, including the king himself, had some trouble swallowing his protestations.

Chapter 5: The Spanish and Aztecs in Tenochtitlán

Having established alliances with several of the coastal peoples, while still remaining in contact with Aztec emissaries and holding out for a requested meeting with Moctezuma, Cortés eventually marched inland toward Tenochtitlán. He departed with about three hundred of his own men, plus several hundred Totonac allies, leaving another hundred or so Spaniards behind in Veracruz. Along the way he encountered another people which had long rejected the legitimacy of Aztec rule: the Tlaxcalans or Tlaxcaltecas. They were a particularly warlike people, as the Spaniards discovered in a series of skirmishes with them. It appears that both groups concluded, after a series of meetings between Spanish and Tlaxcalan emissaries, that each could make use of the other in a common war against the Aztecs.

Although it is not clear at this point that Cortés already intended to undertake an immediate war against Moctezuma and his people, the Tlaxcalan alliance would prove crucial in everything that followed. Indeed, by the time the Spaniards left Tlaxcala, they were accompanied by about 3,000 Tlaxcalan warriors, approximately three times the size of the Spanish force itself. This fact, as historian Matthew Restall has argued, puts to rest the myth of a tiny army of Spaniards defeating a great empire; in reality, the Spanish expedition would have almost certainly been routed without a massive contingent of allies.

With his large assembled forces in tow, Cortés proceeded onward to the city of Cholula, second only to the capital of Tenochtitlán in scale. Its inhabitants were traditionally close allies of the Aztecs and enemies of the Tlaxcalans, so the arrival of a large army of their rivals no doubt caused some unease. Nevertheless, the newcomers were welcomed into the city, and Cortés requested an audience with the king and other notables. What followed was a kind of rehearsal for the treachery and brutality that would then be practiced on a larger scale in the capital. Having invited the chief authorities of the city into a public square, they ambushed the crowd of hundreds of unarmed people gathered there, killing in one audacious stroke the entire leadership of the city as well as much of its warrior class. Cortés subsequently claimed that he had received word, through Doña Marina, that some of the Cholulans were plotting with a nearby Aztec regiment to massacre the Spaniards, and that they had acted in self-defense. Historians find this implausible, and have sought other explanations. One is that the massacre was carried out at the behest of the Tlaxcalans, who had their own agenda to pursue against their rivals. Another is that Cortés's main purpose was to instill fear in the local inhabitants in general and Moctezuma and his advisors in particular.

As the Spanish column entered the mountainous region around the Valley of Mexico on their advance toward the Aztec capital, they met an envoy from Moctezuma named Tzihuacpopocatzin who presented them with gold trinkets, with apparent orders to observe the Spanish reaction to the gift of the precious metal. Again, the description given by Aztec writers differs considerably from that provided by Diaz del Castillo, and the indigenous Mexicans report that the Spanish "hungered like pigs for gold." The Aztec representative's second mission was to attempt to pass himself off as Moctezuma, but this effort was thwarted by the Tlaxcaltecan caciques and troops, who knew the Aztec Huey-tlatoani personally. The Broken Spears also records that at this time, an aspect of the Aztec god Tezcatlipoca–associated with the night sky and winds–appeared to a group of magicians and priests sent to the Spaniards by Moctezuma. The god supposedly appeared as a drunken young man, who asked the messengers what Moctezuma was doing and predicted that Mexico would fall and soon be in flames; when the envoys looked towards Tenochtitlán, it appeared to glow red and orange as though burning. Seeing these signs, the priests and magicians quickly built a temple and small hut for the god, but he soon faded away. The envoys were so disturbed that they did not go forth to meet the conquistadors but returned to Tenochtitlán. It should also be mentioned that Tezcatlipoca was considered the rival and enemy of Quetzalcoatl, so this account may merely be an "after-the-fact" fabrication designed to illustrate Moctezuma's inaction and Cortés deity (as Quetzalcoatl). The encounter also perfectly fits into the Mesoamerican concept of nepantla. Simply put, nepantla is the give-and-take, back-and-forth, and binary reality of human life as the Aztecs (and other Mesoamerican peoples) understood it. Describing their situation after the conquest, surviving Aztecs would often say they were in nepantla; the word was often translated as "chaos," but this is a very simplistic definition for a complex concept.

When the magicians and priests returned to Tenochtitlán and reported to Moctezuma, he despaired saying, "What help is there now, my friends? Is there a mountain for us to climb? Should we run away? We are Mexicanos: would this bring any glory to the Mexican nation? Pity the old men, and the old women, and the innocent little children. How can they save themselves? But there is no help. What can we do? Is there nothing left to us? We will be judged and punished. And however it may be, and whatever it may be, we can do nothing but wait." Moctezuma's reaction may be viewed as a religious one, in light of the "vision" of Tezcatlipoca that was reported to him. The despair he suffered would stem from the understanding that Quetzalcoatl had effectively overcome Tezcatlipoca, and the returning god intended to destroy the city and unseat the Huey-tlatoani.

The conquistadors approached the capital with their indigenous allies and entered the Valley of Mexico. As they descended the mountains, the sprawling valley–filled with cities and towns–lay spreading before them. Some of the conquistadors wanted to return to Tlaxcala and recruit more warriors, but Cortés urged his men onward. They camped in the foothills, and as they continued toward Tenochtitlán the following morning, they were approached by Ixtlilxochitl–a prince from Texcoco–and a large group of his followers. The prince invited the conquistadors into the city and promised to serve the Spaniards in any way possible. Upon entering the city, the Spaniards reported to the inhabitants that they had come only to convert them to Christianity. When the Spanish troops knelt in obeisance to a crucifix, Ixtlilxochitl and those around him did the same, and the prince ad his retinue converted to Christianity on the spot. This might seem to be a flippant conversion, but when one considers that the Aztecs had largely gained control of a huge swath of territory by this method of religious conversion and acceptance. Converting to the faith of a conquering army probably seemed like a normal progression for the people of Texcoco.

As the Spaniards drew nearer, Moctezuma called a meeting with his nephew, Cacama, and his brother, Cuitlahuac, asking for their advice. Cacama suggested that they welcome the Spaniards, saying it would be improper for a great king (Moctezuma) to refuse to welcome the representative from another (King Charles). Cuitlahuac warned his brother that the foreigners should not be welcomed at all because he rightly believed the conquistadors would overthrow the Aztecs. Moctezuma decided to welcome the Spaniards as friends and prepared to meet with Cortés.

Whatever doubts or second thoughts the Spaniards had about undertaking the conquest of the Aztec were dispelled when they laid eyes upon Tenochtitlán. Today Tenochtitlán is mostly remembered for being a floating island city, made all the more ironic by the fact that it was essentially the forerunner of Mexico City, one of the biggest cities in the world today. Lake Texcoco was part of a closed river basin consisting of shallow lakes, lagoons and marshes that formed during the period of glaciation and received additional waters during the annual rainy season. It was on this lake that the floating city was created.

Because the existence of Tenochtitlán depended on water management for the safety of the city, the Aztecs developed ingenius waterworks to facilitate agriculture and the movement of goods. Aqueducts supplied the drinking water, while canals, wharves and flood control gates enabled reliable waterborne commerce. The Aztecs maintained control of the input of water into the lakes and marshes, keeping the salt content of the otherwise closed system under control. Though they accomplished this with hard labor, the Aztecs ensured that Tláloc, the god of water who controlled rain and storms, was content, with one of the two elevated sanctuaries on the great central pyramid of Tenochtitlán was dedicated to Tláloc.

Tlaloc, Codex Rios, after 1566. Vatican Library

Fresh water was first supplied to the city by means of two channels made of reeds and mud that ran from Chapultepec, and reservoirs were constructed in Tenochtitlán from which residents obtained their water for household use. The two channels also delivered water to underground aqueducts that supplied the palaces of the elite in the center of the city. The running water was used to supply the many baths in the palaces, as well as pools and irrigated gardens.

At the height of the Aztec empire, a more ambitious aqueduct was constructed between Chapultepec and the city, spanning nearly 10 miles. This aqueduct was over 20 feet wide. As the city grew further and more water was required, another elaborate aqueduct was constructed in 1499 to bring water from five springs that fed into a dammed basin in Coyoacán. Lacking a control mechanism to prevent exceptional water flow from coursing down the spill way into the city, the aqueduct actually proved to be a hazard to the inhabitants of Tenochtitlán. In 1500, when there were unprecedented rains, the city suffered a disastrous flood partly due to the rising water level in Lake Texcoco but more importantly from this unstoppable aqueduct.

The Aztecs used a considerable amount of water for bathing and washing their streets, with thousands of laborers watering and sweeping the streets daily. The elite classes also kept themselves clean by using soap to bathe, and according to the Spanish, Montezuma bathed twice a day in tubs in the royal palace. He apparently changed his clothes frequently as well.

The Aztecs were meticulous in the control of waste. No solid waste was disposed of through the drainage pipes that emptied into the lake. Care was taken to collect solid waste and what was appropriate was taken to the chiampas for use as fertilizer.

By the time Tenochtitlán was taken by the Spanish, it spanned some 1,000 hectares, the equivalent of 10 million square meters. The incredible size and organization of Tenochtitlán was so impressive to the conquistadors that some of them compared it to Venice. The population size also astonished the conquistadors, who found one well organized market in which 60,000 people were carrying on business. The market had a huge variety of goods for exchange, and nearby were a number of studios where highly skilled artisans worked and sold their goods.

The city centered on the walled square of the Great Temple and adjacent residences of the king, priests and elite warriors. The streets were laid out in a grid pattern interspersed by canals in each of the quarters and their constituent calpulli or wards. Causeways connected the city to the mainland, alongside which ran the aqueducts.

Ruins of Templo Mayor

In the center of Tenochtitlán was a walled precinct. The wall was decorated on the outside with snakes, earning it the name *coatepantli* or serpent wall. It contained a large square, the enormous pyramidal Templo Mayor. The Templo Mayor or Great Temple was rebuilt several times over, with the new and improved structure simply constructed over the previous and less elevated pyramid. The last version of the Templo Mayor was dedicated in 1487 and reached a height of about 130 feet.

The pyramid was capped by two temples, with one dedicated to Huizilopochtli and the other to Tláloc. The idea of capping a pyramid with twin temples was derived from earlier post classic construction at such sites as Tula and Teotihuacán. Though the Mayans are the ones remembered for their mastery of astronomy, the Aztecs' temples were oriented in such a way as to emphasize the seasonal movement of the sun. In the wetter season, the sun rose behind the Temple of Tláloc, and in the summer it rose behind the Temple of Huizilopochtli. On the two equinoctial days the sun rose between the two temples and shone on the Temple of Quetzalcoatl that faced the Templo Mayor.

In the walled central temple enclosure there were five other structures. Among them were the Temple of Xipe Totec and the Temple of Tezcatlipoca. Included in the central temple enclosure was also a ball court where it is presumed religiously based athletic competitions were held. The exact nature of the Aztec ball game is unknown, but it is likely that it was similar to that in other Mesoamerican cities and involved teams hitting a ball through a goal using their hips or chests or heads.

The common people of Tenochtitlán lived in houses that fronted on the streets of their calpulli. The adobe or wattle and daub houses were L-shaped, enclosing an interior courtyard in which most of the domestic activities were carried out. Here the women spun thread and wove fabric, ground corn, baked tortillas, prepared food and interacted with kin who came and went with little formality. The domestic court was the site of family festivals celebrating the birth or naming of a child, in which quantities of food were given to friends, neighbors and the hungry poor. The common men worked on their chinampas or fished in the lake.

Estimates of the population of Tenochtitlán vary considerably, but it is likely that the total population of the city was in the range of 200,000 to 300,000 most of which would have been of the common class. It is probable that the second largest segment of the population were slaves. The sheer number of people in Tenochtitlán amazed the conquistadors, who compared the size of the city to some of the largest municipalities at home in Spain. Incredibly, the city had amenities that were unthought of even in Europe. For example, there were schools for children of all classes, even commoners. Adjacent to the local temple the schools provided instruction for children from 7 to 14 years in age with boys and girls taught in separate rooms. Children were taught the history of the Aztecs, dancing, singing, public speaking and were even given religious instruction. The schools for children of the elite were located in the center of Tenochtitlán. There they were taught a broader curriculum that included astronomy, arithmetic, oratory, reading and writing.

The priestly and elite warrior class dwelt in more luxurious palaces located near the royal palace around the central temple precinct. These buildings were presumably highly decorated with relief sculptures and may have been colorfully painted outside and inside.

The king lived on the second floor of his palace with two wives and 150 concubines as well as a great number of servants, guards and attendants. To feed this vast crowd the palace had extensive kitchens and store rooms. Celebratory banquets included a variety of tempting dishes, including frogs with green peppers, sage locusts and nopal with fish eggs. As many as 300 guests were fed at special banquets. While the king ate with his guests, he was hidden behind a screen during the meal.

The highly stratified society of the Aztecs involved the regulation of various rights and privileges of the inhabitants of Tenochtitlán. For example, Montezuma I enacted a series of precise sumptuary laws prohibiting commoners from wearing cotton or a cloak falling below the knee. Commoners were also forbidden to wear sandals in the city streets, while specific kinds of cloaks, jewels and decoration were prescribed as appropriate to various levels of society and different ranks of warriors.

When Cortés and his men arrived in Tenochtitlán, it was probably larger than any European city of the era. Bernal Díaz, who accompanied Cortés, described the reaction of the Spanish soldiers as they first approached the great city: "We saw so many cities and villages built both on the water and on dry land, and a straight, level causeway (to Tenochtitlán), we couldn't resist our admiration. It was like the enchantments in the book of Amadis (de Gaula, a popular Spanish chivalric romance of the late middle ages), because of the high towers, pyramids and other buildings, all of masonry, which rose from the water. Some of our soldiers asked if what we saw was not a dream."

This was the first great urban civilization that the Spaniards, who had initially come to the Americas seeking the rich and sophisticated kingdoms of Asia, encountered in the New World. Within less than two years of the first arrival of the Spanish there, Tenochtitlán would be in ruins.

The combined Spanish and Tlaxcalan force of several thousand entered the Aztec capital on November 8, 1519. They were prepared for battle, but initially met a peaceful reception. Moctezuma, as he had previously done on several occasions through emissaries, presented the visitors with lavish gifts, including objects forged from gold, which surely whetted the Spaniards' appetite. They were welcomed into the city and brought into its central palace complex. When the two leaders met, Moctezuma spoke first, addressing Cortés as though he was Quetzalcoatl and saying that the throne was his and had only been cared for by the Huey-tlatoani and his predecessors. Moctezuma was quoted as saying, "You have graciously come on earth, you have graciously approached your water, your high place of Mexico, you have come down to your mat, your throne, which I have briefly kept for you, I who used to keep it for you…You have graciously arrived, you have known pain, you have known weariness, now come on earth, take your rest, enter into your palace, rest your limbs; may our lords come on earth." While this seems to be the ultimate sign of deference, some scholars note that Moctezuma's polite speech was intended to be his way of asserting dominance and demonstrating his superiority.

Of course, if that was the message Moctezuma meant to convey, the conquistadors did not get it. Cortés, in a typically deceptive statement delivered through Doña Marina said, "Tell Moctezuma that we are his friends. There is nothing to fear. We have wanted to see him for a long time, and now we have seen his face and heard his words. Tell him that we love him well and that our hearts are contented." Then directly to Moctezuma he said, "We have come to your house in Mexico as friends. There is nothing to fear." Moctezuma was accompanied by several other Aztec lords and chiefs.

Many have wondered why an apparently hostile army was treated with such hospitality, especially after the massacre at Cholula. One theory is that Moctezuma simply did not imagine that such a small force could be a threat to his enormous city. Once the strangers were ensconced in the city, he may have reasoned, they were trapped and would have great difficulty escaping.

Hernan Cortés and La Malinche meet Moctezuma II in Tenochtitlán, November 8, 1519. Facsimile (c. 1890) of Lienzo de Tlaxcala.

When the Spaniards gained entry to the royal palaces, they immediately placed Moctezuma under guard, effectively imprisoning him in his own palace. As this was done, other members of the Spanish expedition wandered about the city, examining everything they saw, no doubt searching for gold, and that evening, they fired one of their cannons which caused great confusion and fear among the residents of Tenochtitlán. The following morning, the Spaniards issued orders to Moctezuma, requesting various foodstuffs, which he passed along to chiefs to fulfill. This angered the chiefs ordered to comply, who began to feel that their Huey-tlatoani was both being dishonored and submitting to a band of foreign barbarians. The Spaniards then began questioning Moctezuma about the city and its resources, finally coming to their actual point: the location of the gold. As the conquistadors escorted Moctezuma to the Aztec treasury, they surrounded him with armed men, walking in a tight circle around the Huey-tlatoani. When the Spaniards were shown various emblems and shields made of feathers and gold, they seized them as if they were their own and stripped away all but the precious metal they sought. Aztec commentators noted that the Spanish wanted only the gold and discarded things that the Mesoamericans considered very valuable (such as quetzal feathers). The conquistadors then demanded to be shown Moctezuma's personal treasures, and when they were taken there, they again fell on the gold and began piling it on a nearby patio without consideration for it ownership and acting as though they had found it by pure luck. At this point, Doña Marina called the Aztec nobles together and exhorted them to help the Spaniards, to feed them and bring them water, finally asking why the Aztecs shied away from the foreigners, asking whether the Aztecs were angry with the conquistadors. But, according to The Broken Spears, "the Mexicans were too frightened to approach. They were crushed by terror and would not risk coming forward. They shied away as if the Spaniards were wild beasts, as if the hour were midnight on the blackest night of the year. Yet they did not abandon the Spaniards to hunger and thirst. They brought them whatever they needed, but shook with fear as they did so."

For several months, Cortés essentially ruled Tenochtitlán through the authority of his captive, not establishing decisive control there but biding his time until a more forceful move could be taken. However, Cortés still had the authorities of his own government to deal with as well. In April 1520, a Spanish expedition of around 1,000 men under the command of Pánfilo de Narváez was sent out by Governor Velázquez from Cuba with orders to subdue Cortés. Here again Cortés was severely outnumbered, but his ruthlessness won out. Leaving Tenochtitlán and heading for the coast, Cortés feigned a desire to enter into peace talks, holding out a promise of consensual submission to the governor's authority. All the while, he was planning to attack and sending messengers to Narváez's camp with bribes and promises of rewards if they mutinied against their appointed leader. Narváez was unprepared when Cortés and his men descended on the encampment fully armed and ready to fight. He was forced to surrender and fell captive to his enemy, who left him imprisoned in Veracruz while leading off a large contingent of his soldiers back toward Tenochtitlán. It is an interesting fact that Cortés did not reserve his treacherous disregard for basic honesty for his interactions with the natives. He behaved with similar callousness toward his own people, albeit with much less brutality, but even that might have been only because he did not have to resort to brute force.

Chapter 6: The Death of Moctezuma and the Demise of the Aztec Empire

More is known about Aztec religious practices than any other aspect of their culture, mostly because the major element in the public ceremonies was focused on human sacrifice. The rituals were apparently so gruesome that they horrified even the Spanish, who were not exactly known for their gentility when it came to war and religious fervor. And ultimately, it would be those practices that served as the Spaniards' pretext for the chain of events that resulted in the controversial death of Moctezuma himself.

Some time after Moctezuma was taken prisoner by the Spaniards and Cortés had left the capital, a delegation of worshippers approached the Aztec ruler and asked permission to conduct the annual Feast of Toxcatl, a feast honoring the Aztec's main god Huitzilopochtli. The Huey-tlatoani granted their request and preparations for the celebration began. The conquistadors expressed interest in this fiesta and stated that they wished to observe the proceedings.

A statue of Huitzilopochtli was fashioned from a paste of chicolote (an edible seed) molded over a wooden framework. On the appointed day, worshippers approached the statue and left offerings of seed cakes and human flesh for the god. The celebrants were mainly warriors of all ages and ranks; those most senior warriors led the younger, less experienced dancers. Huitzilopochtli was the god of war, and the warriors danced in files, with the experienced warriors at the head of these files, with rank and experience decreasing as one moved down the file. A drummer set the beat and soon the dancers were moving in graceful unison, to the rhythm of the drum.

At this point in the celebration, the Spaniards rushed into the patio where the dancers were, sealed the exits and began slaughtering the unarmed warriors. They first cut off the arms of the drummer, followed quickly by his head. The patio broke into chaos, and soon, all the dancers lay dead, hacked to pieces by the murderous conquistadores. Diaz del Castillo glosses over this event, implying that it had been undertaken to subdue the Aztecs, employing the saying "He who attacks first gains the victory." The Spaniards continued searching throughout the celebratory complex, seeking further victims and killing all they encountered.

Cortés's lieutenant Pedro de Alvarado was immediately responsible for planning and ordering the attack, but it is not clear whether he was acting under orders from his superior or on his own initiative. Some speculate that Cortés deliberately planned for it to occur during his absence so that he could claim to have been uninvolved. They are thought to have killed thousands, possibly as many as eight thousand, that day, primarily using swords, spears, and knives. As in Cholula, the perpetrators later claimed that they had gotten wind of a plot against them by the Aztecs; they also claimed that they were acting to prevent the participants in the festival from carrying out rituals involving human sacrifice and cannibalism.

Pedro de Alvarado

The Aztecs clearly had a stomach for blood and death, but the massacre during a celebratory festival by the Spaniards definitively exhausted their toleration of the invaders, who despite the thousands they killed were still outnumbered and highly vulnerable under siege. As news of the massacre spread through the city, a great roar of outrage rose and the Aztecs attacked the Spaniards fiercely, forcing them to retreat to the relative safety of Moctezuma's palace. The conquistadors took up positions and began firing at the attacking Aztecs with their crossbows, cannons, and arquebuses. They also shackled Moctezuma, and the Huey-tlatoani ordered one of his ministers, Itzcuauhtzin, to address the Aztecs, asking them to stop attacking the Spaniards. Itzcuauhtzin told the people that they were no match for the Spaniards and that the old would be the ones to suffer, delivering all of this in Moctezuma's name. The enraged Aztecs replied by insulting the speaker and screaming, "Who is Moctezuma to give us orders? We are no longer his slaves?" The attacks continued and the Spaniards were effectively besieged within the royal palace, and the gathered crowds refused to disperse or give up their weapons. The Aztecs sealed the area around the palace grounds and began seizing servants attempting to bring food or supplies to the royal household, naming them traitors and killing some.

When Cortés and the men accompanying him arrived, they found the city's streets deserted and the population openly hostile. What ensued was a kind of prototype of urban guerrilla warfare.

In the tight, enclosed spaces of the city, the Spaniards' horses were of little advantage, and their weapons could not be fired effectively. Within a short period, it became clear that they had lost their advantage, and they were running low on food and artillery. Cortés's gambit was to have Moctezuma, still his captive, speak to his people, ostensibly in the hope of a further reconciliation.

On the third day of the siege, Moctezuma, almost certainly forced to do so by the conquistadors, mounted the roof of the palace and tried to address the crowds. However, the angered Aztecs cursed him, calling him a coward and traitor to his country. According to Diaz del Castillo, the Huey-tlatoani was killed by arrows and a sling stone which struck his head: "Barely was [the emperor's speech to his subjects] finished when a sudden shower of stones and darts descended. Our men who had been shielding Montezuma had momentarily neglected their duty when they saw the attack cease while he spoke to his chiefs. Montezuma was hit by three stones, one on the head, one on the arm, and one on the leg; and though they begged him to have his wounds dressed and eat some food and spoke very kindly to him, he refused. Then quite unexpectedly we were told that he was dead."

Naturally, indigenous accounts vary drastically from the Spanish account. The Aztec writers cited in *The Broken Spears* reference Diaz's account ("it is said that an Indian killed him with a stone from his sling."), but that statement is followed by a comment citing palace servants who allegedly witnessed the Aztec ruler being stabbed in the abdomen by the Spaniards. Either way, Moctezuma was killed during the siege, which would last another four days. Given the duplicitous nature of the conquistadors, modern scholars have tended to believe the indigenous accounts over the Spanish accounts.

The retreat that followed after Moctezuma's death has become known as the *Noche triste* ("sad night," "night of sorrow"), although the Aztecs were presumably not sorry to see the Spaniards go or even terribly sorry for the loss of their ineffectual ruler. Cortés and his men, knowing they were badly outnumbered and had little chance of surviving open combat in the city, chose to flee after sending a false message of truce to their enemies. They fled in the middle of the night, aiming for the most deserted causeway leading out of the city and across the lake, but the retreat still went disastrously. It began to rain heavily, thunderstorms added to their consternation, and all out chaos ensued when they were attacked by large numbers of their opponents, who had been alerted to their movements. Many of the Spaniards were weighted down with gold and other loot from the city and drowned when they tried to swim away from the causeway, while others were simply killed by the attackers. All in all, hundreds of them did not escape the city alive, leaving the force greatly diminished. By the time Cortés reached the shores of the lake, he had lost most of his army and much of the treasure he and his men had taken from Moctezuma's palace. His initial plan to take control of the Aztec empire by stealth, keeping Moctezuma on the throne as a nominal leader while ruling from behind the scenes, had failed disastrously. Now he would need to try a different and far more dramatic strategy.

Even after clearing the causeway, the retreating Spaniards were pursued by their Aztec enemies and engaged in repeated skirmishes as they fled toward Tlaxcala to reconvene with allies there. In the valley of Otumba, they were attacked by a large Aztec force and a bloody battle followed. Despite being outnumbered, the Spaniards ultimately beat back their opponents, partly because of the superior speed and agility provided by their horses, which had proved much less of an asset in the urban setting of Tenochtitlán. Their equivocal victory at Otumba allowed them to proceed on toward the east, but they lost many more men, both Spaniards and native allies, in the fighting. By the time they arrived in Tlaxcala, nearly 900 Spanish soldiers and more than a thousand native allies had perished. In their weakened position and having failed in their first campaign, the Spaniards were in a weaker bargaining position with their allies, who demanded further concessions in exchange for continued support. Cortés was willing to grant the Tlaxcalans much of what they requested, including control of previously held Aztec territories as tributary regions, and partial control of Tenochtitlán itself. In exchange, he obtained an army of allies who had even more stake in victory and thus higher morale.

Thinking that the Spaniards would not return to their city, the Aztecs rejoiced, and a council of four Aztec lords elected Cuitlahuac, Moctezuma's surviving brother, as the new Huey-tlatoani. But the Aztec still had several issues to deal with. First, Tenochtitlán had been left in a chaotic state, and although Cuitláhuac had been appointed as a successor for Moctezuma, his authority was not yet fully consolidated. Traditionally Aztec rulers were required to demonstrate their prowess by leading an army into battle and taking captives, who would then be sacrificed to the gods upon his return. The military venture would also serve the purpose of confirming his effective leadership and obtaining the continued loyalty of tributary states. However appropriate it may have seemed to take an army to Tlaxcala to confront the Spaniards and their allies there, Cuitláhuac was formally prohibited from leading a full military campaign because the season for such activities had not yet arrived: most able-bodied men were supposed to be harvesting food rather than fighting. Only when the winter came would it be possible to assemble a large military force.

On the other hand, there was a certain strategic advantage to remaining in Tenochtitlán, since it seemed an easy position to fortify and defend given its location on the lake: any advancing army would have to cross the narrow causeways, and as the Spaniards had already discovered, this would make them easy targets. For one of these reasons, or perhaps all of them, the Aztecs hung back for the moment, as did the Spaniards, who sent for reinforcements from Veracruz and Cuba and went about building support from several smaller cities in the Tlaxcalan sphere of influence.

By the time the Aztecs sent out expeditionary forces to attack the Spaniards in the Fall of 1520, the Spaniards had gathered an impressive array of support from native allied forces, and their own resources had augmented thanks to a growing trickle of soldiers, horses, and artillery arriving from the Gulf of Mexico. Still, the army that finally gathered to re-enter the Valley of Mexico toward the end of that same year was less than 5% Spanish, and it is unlikely that most of the native soldiers who participated regarded themselves as under Cortés's command. The traditional view of the "Spanish Conquest" thus needs to be revised. Although the Spaniards ultimately derived the most benefit from the war against the Aztecs, most of the participants in the successful campaign were neither Spanish nor conquerors: they were pursuing an agenda that would ostensibly increase their city's share of regional power.

Just as importantly, a terrible plague began to sweep through the Aztec capital. It was smallpox borne by the Spanish invaders, and among its first victims was the new Huey-tlatoani himself, Cuitlahuac. Smallpox caused massive devastation throughout the city, as thousands succumbed to a disease against which none had any resistance, and as many died from hunger as died from the actual effects of the disease. Subsequent waves of smallpox occurred over the following months and diminished in intensity as time passed, but the damage had been done and the population had been decimated. Cuitlahuac had died in December, meaning that the Aztecs were without a leader at a time in which they should have been marshaling forces for war. The succession was controversial, and the next chosen king, Cuahtemoc, was not officially recognized until February of 1521. By this time, the Spaniards had returned and had a number of new advantages.

With a greatly enlarged contingent of native allies, hundreds of reinforcements from Cuba, and a refreshed stock of arquebuses, cannons, and gunpowder, Cortés now headed toward Tenochtitlán with a far superior force than he had previously. Even still, he did not proceed immediately to the city but set out to consolidate his control of the surrounding region, establishing alliances where possible and subduing cities and towns where necessary. The aim was to isolate the Aztecs, cut off their supplies of food and fresh water from neighboring territories, and prevent them from being able to summon reinforcements. The strategy was effective, and the result was a tightening noose around the already diminished, divided, and illness-ravaged Aztec populations. Cortés also arrived at Lake Texcoco with brigantines that allowed his forces to cross the lake and attack the city without needing to use the causeways. But for the most part, he and his allies waged a defensive war.

Once the supply chain had been cut off and food and water were scarce in the city, the Aztecs' only recourse was to go out and try to fend off the siege, thus leaving themselves vulnerable to attacks from their enemies. But despite mass starvation, the Aztecs held out and continued to prevent any major advances on their city for months.

Finally, in July, the Spaniards and their allies managed to gain a foothold on the island, and proceeded to make their way through the city, razing structures to the ground to prevent ambushes. Worn down by illness, starvation, thirst, and relentless arquebus and cannon attacks, the Aztecs held out until August 13, 1521, the day Cuahtemoc was captured. He reportedly surrendered directly to Cortés, but his surrender was not recognized and he was taken prisoner and ultimately executed. The total numbers are uncertain, but Aztec casualties from the siege, including the deaths of warriors in battle and deaths from illness, starvation, and massacres of civilians, reached the hundreds of thousands. In the latest stage of their campaign, the Spaniards had lost perhaps 500 and native allies had perished in the tens of thousands.

Within less than two years, the Aztec empire had been destroyed, with their population decimated and their great capital left in ruins. Cortés proceeded to take credit for the entire enterprise, but in reality his success was highly dependent on the enormous assistance he received from his local allies. Perhaps more than a great military strategist, he had again shown himself to be a consummate politician.

Chapter 7: Cortés after the Conquest

Cortés would live more than 20 years after the conquest, and during those years his example would inspire many other Spaniards to seek their fortune in a similar way. The most successful of them was probably Francisco Pizarro, Cortés's second cousin, who would soon overcome an even larger empire to the south.

Pizarro

Cortés, on the other hand, would continue to reap benefits from his success, but his position would never again be quite as spectacular as it was in the wake of his defeat of the Aztecs. Although he had begun his campaign in a nearly treasonous manner, Charles V proved willing to forgive him his transgressions once he realized the wealth and scale of the newly subdued territory. He appointed Cortés governor of the entire Aztec empire, a position he was happy to assume since he no longer regarded his promises to allied native leaders as binding now once reinforcements were flooding in from Spain. The new name of the territory was to be New Spain. Cortés invited Franciscan friars to evangelize the population, and he began to establish the same *encomienda* system of labor practiced in the island territories. He continued the demolition of Aztec Tenochtitlán and began to build what would become Mexico City.

Once established firmly at the helm of the new colony, Cortés had no scruples about reneging on his promises to native allies, and he treated his own men nearly as poorly in some cases. They had come enticed by promises of wealth, but instead found themselves in debt to Cortés, who charged them for their use of weaponry he had supplied and for food, drink, and medical care. Meanwhile, merchants flooded in from Europe, selling goods at inflated prices. The disappointment suffered by many of those who fought with Cortés created a conflicted and tense environment and weakened the new governor's authority, even though it may have enriched him in the short term. Several of his former lieutenants set out on conquering expeditions on their own, hoping to recoup their losses and establish themselves independently as Cortés himself had done. One of them, Cristóbal de Olid, conspired with Cortés's old nemesis Diego Velázquez to take control of Honduras and rule it as his own territory. The attempt enraged Cortés, who had Olid captured and relieved of his command, but the conflict began a series of intrigues that pitted Cortés once more against Velázquez. Cortés clearly knew how to play the game, but Velázquez had far more influence in the Spanish court. The ultimate result was that Cortés was relieved of his governorship, exiled from the territory he had conquered, and sent back to Spain in 1528.

Cortés's remaining years were marked by repeated reversals of fortune. Sent back to Spain in a humiliating state, he was able to gain an audience with the crown. Successfully defending himself against various charges levelled by his enemies and rivals, he was honored by the king with a new title – Marquis of the Valley of Oaxaca – and a large *encomienda* in one of the wealthiest regions of New Spain. Despite these successes, he found himself with a reduced political stature when he returned to Mexico, not only because he was resented by many but because the crown, which was in the process of centralizing control over its American holdings, probably did not trust someone with his demonstrated ambitions to hold power responsibly. Already, the free-wheeling period of colonization in which he had taken part was giving way to the viceregal period, in which Spain would govern its overseas territories through a centralized and bureacratic administration in which individualists like Cortés would no longer thrive. In the late 1530s, perhaps attempting to relive his earlier triumphs, he set out on an expedition up the Pacific Coast, where he became among the first Europeans to reach Baja California.

Partly due to a conflict over his rights over the newly discovered territories and partly due to the lack of obvious wealth to be exploited there, Cortés eventually returned to central Mexico and then to Spain. His new exploratory mission had earned him a new crop of enemies in Mexico, and he probably hoped to obtain further support from the king. Instead, he received little recognition from Charles V, who was consumed with several wars in Europe and not terribly interested in his American holdings. In an attempt to win back the good grace of the sovereign, in 1541 he joined an expedition across the Mediterranean against the enemy Ottoman Empire, but a subsequent attack on Algiers led to a disastrous rout of the Spanish forces, and Cortés barely escaped with his life. He lived much of the rest of his life racked with debts and embittered about his lack of recognition. He attempted to return to Mexico in late 1547, but fell ill in the port of Seville, where he died on December 2, 1547.

Charles V

Chapter 8: The Legacy of Cortés

A curious myth that sprung up in the immediate aftermath of his death claimed that Hernán Cortés, the conqueror of Mexico, had both been born and died on the same day and hour as Martin Luther, the founder of Protestantism. Moreover, this myth asserted, Cortés and Luther had led precisely parallel careers: while Luther had led much of Europe away from the Roman Catholic Church, Cortés had brought the people of a new continent into the Catholic fold; while

Luther's reforms had deprived the Church of much of its property in Northern Europe, Cortés's conquest had filled the Church's coffers with untold quantities of gold.

As bizarre as it may appear at first, it is clear why such a myth made sense to the embattled Catholic Church of the mid-sixteenth century, which had recently, with the Protestant Reformation, felt its supremacy challenged from within for the first time in almost a thousand years. The parallel lives of Luther and Cortés proved that even though Satan was succeeding in undermining the Church through footsoldiers like Luther, God was counteracting the damage by way of appointed defenders of the faith such as Cortés. The latter's deeds were taken as proof of God's providential plan for human history, which would lead ultimately to universal salvation.

The Cortés-Luther legend provides a vivid index of the deeply theological worldview of Christian Europe in the Age of Exploration, the period in which Cortés played such a pivotal role. The new – in this case, in the form of the new lands being explored and conquered in the New World, and the new faiths springing up in a formerly united Christendom – had to be incorporated into traditional frameworks so that it would confirm the teleological and apocalyptic Christian narrative that had long been promulgated by the Church and accepted in some form by most Europeans. In his book *The Old World and the New*, historian J.H. Elliott argues that it took some centuries for the genuine newness and difference of the Americas to be registered by European culture, so intent were most observers on finding ways of incorporating all new data into familiar narrative structures. Similarly, it can obviously be pointed out that it took some time for Cortés's career to be assessed historically, rather than theologically and morally.

On the other hand, there are some striking continuities between the initial accounts of Cortés's life that sprung up in his time and modern views of him: Protestants, for the most part, saw him as a villain and a scoundrel, proof of the tyrannical and brutal ways of the Catholic world at large, while many Catholics saw him as a hero of the faith. A similar split persists to this day: he is greatly despised for his ruthlessness, cunning, and dishonesty in many quarters, but for many still remains a heroic figure and paragon of remarkable individual accomplishments. Although Cortés was in fact born two years later than Luther and died more than a year after the famous reformer, the strange legend of their parallel lives contains the seed of an insight that most historians would accept today. Both Luther and Cortés were undoubtedly pivotal figures in the making of the modern world. Both struck out decisively beyond the horizons of medieval Catholicism and did so with a disregard of traditional authorities and hierarchies that set them apart from many of their peers. Both played a significant role in begetting a new culture: Luther, the individualistic, literate, and anti-hierarchical culture of Protestant Northern Europe, and Cortés, the conflicted but vital cultural and racial blend that would ultimately become modern Mexico and Latin America. Both also propelled the development of modern global capitalism: Luther, by fomenting a religious culture more propitious to the ambitions of merchants, traders, and moneylenders, and Cortés, by injecting the precious metals of the New World into the world economy. All in all, while they may have been regarded as opposite figures in their time, any account of the birth of the modern, globalized world that exists today could regard their roles as complementary.

While Cortés was certainly one of the most important figures in the history of the last millennium, he remains a difficult figure to admire as an individual, even if his daring and defiance are impressive. His personality was essentially that of a gambler, with all of the greed, egotism, and unscrupulousness that that suggests. The scion of a Spanish culture that claimed to venerate honor above all things, Cortés was remarkably short on that quality, and his success as a conqueror must be attributed in part to his willingness to break even the most basic rules of decency to achieve political and military victory. Throughout his career, he cheated, deceived, and manipulated those he wished to gain advantage over, and showed himself repeatedly willing to use deadly force against unarmed, friendly interlocutors. He even ripped off his own men, who had loyally and bravely followed him on a highly dangerous expedition. Indeed, as one historian has asserted, "Cortés's actions embodied the political concepts developed by Machiavelli" (Pastor 83).

It is impossible that Cortés could have read Machiavelli's seminal political treatise *The Prince*, but he seemed to have developed a parallel understanding of politics as a ruthless game of deception and cunning all on his own. In fact, his disregard for traditional morality and lack of scruples about the pursuit of worldly power makes him a progenitor of what has later come to be called *Realpolitik*.

Chapter 9: The Legacy of Moctezuma and the Aztecs

Cortes and his men may have quickly conquered the Aztecs and put an end to their empire, but he never could erase their existence. The magnificence of the Aztec civilization that Cortez and his Spanish colonial followers tried so hard to obliterate from history has remained an essential part of modern Mexican identity. The current national flag of Mexico, adopted in 1984, bears the Aztec pictogram for Tenochtitlán. It shows an eagle devouring a snake perched atop a cactus with ripe prickly pears. The cactus grows on an abstract rectangular island.

The flag is one glaring reminder of the fact that Mexico City, one of the largest cities in the world, was built up out of Tenochtitlán's ashes, in a sense carrying on the Aztecs' legacy. In recognition of that fact, some of the city's landmarks and districts still have Nahuatl names, using the Aztecs' own language. Furthermore, the non-human staples of the Aztec diet continue to be prominently featured in Mexico, and now across the entire world, from maize to tortillas. Fittingly, some of these foods continue to go by their original Nahuatl names.

Beyond honoring their Aztec heritage in these ways, Mexicans are fond of celebrating their ancestral roots by dressing up as Aztecs and performing dances that are intended to recall those of their forefathers. Recreational and competitive Aztec dancing is a part of national celebration in many communities.

It is significant in the context of the evolution of modern Mexican national identity that the most important contribution to understanding Aztec civilization was inaugurated in 1978 as a huge, government sponsored project. In that year municipal workers in Mexico City by chance municipal unearthed a enormous stone disk with a relief of the dismemberment of the Aztec moon goddess. The nation was enthralled by this discovery. Thus began a major excavation of the site that has since revealed the remains of the temple precinct of Tenochtitlán and yielded thousands of artifacts that are now housed in a museum adjacent to the ruins.

That the government of Mexico spent so much of the Mexican taxpayers' money to reveal more of the city underneath the center of the modern capital is perhaps the strongest indicator that this once glorious civilization forged the foundation of a modern nation.

In the same vein, regardless of how effective a leader he was or was not, Moctezuma has become a poignant symbol of resistance. Even today, some Native Americans have named deities after Moctezuma, and some tribes have invoked a myth that he will return in vindication some day. It's believed that Montezuma is part of the pantheon of the Tohono O'odham in Northern Mexico and even some of the Pueblo tribes in New Mexico and Arizona. When some indigenous leaders rebelled against European authority in the Americas during the 18th century, they invoked Moctezuma's name as inspiration for their rebellion, including Mayan leader Jacinto Canek, who allegedly referred to himself as "Little Montezuma".

Cortes's Second Letter to Charles V

In his "Second Letter" to Charles V, dated October 30, 1520, Cortés provides perhaps the most descriptive firsthand account of Tenochtitlán and the Aztec people:

IN ORDER, most potent Sire, to convey to your Majesty a just conception of the great extent of this noble city of Temixtitlan, and of the many rare and wonderful objects it contains; of the government and dominions of Moctezuma, the sovereign: of the religious rights and customs that prevail, and the order that exists in this as well as the other cities appertaining to his realm: it would require the labor of many accomplished writers, and much time for the completion of the task. I shall not be able to relate an hundredth part of what could be told respecting these matters; but I will endeavor to describe, in the best manner in my power, what I have myself seen; and imperfectly as I may succeed in the attempt, I am fully aware that the account will appear so wonderful as to be deemed scarcely worthy of credit; since even we who have seen these things with our own eyes, are yet so amazed as to be unable to comprehend their reality. But your Majesty may be assured that if there is any fault in my relation, either in regard to the present subject, or to any other matters of which I shall give your Majesty an account, it will arise from too great brevity rather than extravagance or prolixity in the details; and it seems to me but just to my Prince and Sovereign to declare the truth in the clearest manner, without saying anything that would detract from it, or add to it.

Before I begin to describe this great city and the others already mentioned, it may be well for the better understanding of the subject to say something of the configuration of Mexico, in which they are situated, it being the principal seat of Moctezuma's power. This Province is in the form of a circle, surrounded on all sides by lofty and rugged mountains; its level surface comprises an area of about seventy leagues in circumference, including two lakes, that overspread nearly the whole valley, being navigated by boats more than fifty leagues round. One of these lakes contains fresh and the other, which is the larger of the two, salt water. On one side of the lakes, in the middle of the valley, a range of highlands divides them from one another, with the exception of a narrow strait which lies between the highlands and the lofty sierras. This strait is a bow-shot wide, and connects the two lakes; and by this means a trade is carried on between the cities and other settlements on the lakes in canoes without the necessity of traveling by land. As the salt lake rises and falls with its tides like the sea, during the time of high water it pours into the other lake with the rapidity of a powerful stream; and on the other hand, when the tide has ebbed, the water runs from the fresh into the salt lake.

This great city of Temixtitlan [Mexico] is situated in this salt lake, and from the main land to the denser parts of it, by whichever route one chooses to enter, the distance is two leagues. There are four avenues or entrances to the city, all of which are formed by artificial causeways, two spears' length in width. The city is as large as Seville or Cordova; its streets, I speak of the principal ones, are very wide and straight; some of these, and all the inferior ones, are half land and half water, and are navigated by canoes. All the streets at intervals have openings, through which the water flows, crossing from one street to another; and at these openings, some of which are very wide, there are also very wide bridges, composed of large pieces of timber, of great strength and well put together; on many of these bridges ten horses can go abreast. Foreseeing that if the inhabitants of the city should prove treacherous, they would possess great advantages from the manner in which the city is constructed, since by removing the bridges at the entrances, and abandoning the place, they could leave us to perish by famine without our being able to reach the main land, as soon as I had entered it, I made great haste to build four brigatines, which were soon finished, and were large enough to take ashore three hundred men and the horses, whenever it should become necessary.

This city has many public squares, in which are situated the markets and other places for buying and selling. There is one square twice as large as that of the city of Salamanca, surrounded by porticoes, where are daily assembled more than sixty thousand souls, engaged in buying and selling; and where are found all kinds of merchandise that the world affords, embracing the necessaries of life, as for instance articles of food, as well as jewels of gold and silver, lead, brass, copper, tin, precious stones, bones, shells, snails, and feathers. There are also exposed for sale wrought and unwrought stone, bricks burnt and unburnt, timber hewn and unhewn, of different sorts. There is a street for game, where every variety of birds in the country are sold, as fowls, partridges, quails, wild ducks, fly-catchers, widgeons, turtledoves, pigeons, reed-birds, parrots, sparrows, eagles, hawks, owls, and kestrels; they sell likewise the skins of some birds of prey, with their feathers, head, beak, and claws. There are also sold rabbits, hares, deer, and little dogs [i.e., the chihuahua], which are raised for eating. There is also an herb street, where may be obtained all sorts of roots and medicinal herbs that the country affords. There are apothecaries' shops, where prepared medicines, liquids, ointments, and plasters are sold; barbers' shops, where they wash and shave the head; and restaurateurs, that furnish food and drink at a certain price. There is also a class of men like those called in Castile porters, for carrying burdens. Wood and coal are seen in abundance, and braziers of earthenware for burning coals; mats of various kinds for beds, others of a lighter sort for seats, and for halls and bedrooms.

There are all kinds of green vegetables, especially onions, leeks, garlic, watercresses, nasturtium, borage, sorrel, artichokes, and golden thistle; fruits also of numerous descriptions, amongst which are cherries and plums, similar to those in Spain; honey and wax from bees, and from the stalks of maize, which are as sweet as the sugar-cane; honey is also extracted from the plant called maguey, which is superior to sweet or new wine; from the same plant they extract sugar and wine, which they also sell. Different kinds of cotton thread of all colors in skeins are exposed for sale in one quarter of the market, which has the appearance of the silk-market at Granada, although the former is supplied more abundantly. Painters' colors, as numerous as can be found in Spain, and as fine shades; deerskins dressed and undressed, dyed different colors; earthen-ware of a large size and excellent quality; large and small jars, jugs, pots, bricks, and endless variety of vessels, all made of fine clay, and all or most of them glazed and painted; maize or Indian corn, in the grain and in the form of bread, preferred in the grain for its flavor to that of the other islands and terra-firma; patés of birds and fish; great quantities of fish---fresh, salt, cooked and uncooked; the eggs of hens, geese, and of all the other birds I have mentioned, in great abundance, and cakes made of eggs; finally, everything that can be found throughout the whole country is sold in the markets, comprising articles so numerous that to avoid prolixity, and because their names are not retained in my memory, or are unknown to me, I shall not attempt to enumerate them.

Every kind of merchandise is sold in a particular street or quarter assigned to it exclusively, and thus the best order is preserved. They sell everything by number or measure; at least so far we have not observed them to sell anything by weight. There is a building in the great square that is used as an audience house, where ten or twelve persons, who are magistrates, sit and decide all controversies that arise in the market, and order delinquents to be punished. In the same square there are other persons who go constantly about among the people observing what is sold, and the measures used in selling; and they have been seen to break measures that were not true.

This great city contains a large number of temples, or houses, for their idols, very handsome edifices, which are situated in the different districts and the suburbs; in the principal ones religious persons of each particular sect are constantly residing, for whose use, besides the houses containing the idols, there are other convenient habitations. All these persons dress in black, and never cut or comb their hair from the time they enter the priesthood until they leave it; and all the sons of the principal inhabitants, both nobles and respectable citizens, are placed in the temples and wear the same dress from the age of seven or eight years until they are taken out to be married; which occurs more frequently with the first-born who inherit estates than with the others. The priests are debarred from female society, nor is any woman permitted to enter the religious houses. They also abstain from eating certain kinds of food, more at some seasons of the year than others.

Among these temples there is one which far surpasses all the rest, whose grandeur of architectural details no human tongue is able to describe; for within its precincts, surrounded by a lofty wall, there is room enough for a town of five hundred families. Around the interior of the enclosure there are handsome edifices, containing large halls and corridors, in which the religious persons attached to the temple reside. There are fully forty towers, which are lofty and well built, the largest of which has fifty steps leading to its main body, and is higher than the tower of the principal tower of the church at Seville. The stone and wood of which they are constructed are so well wrought in every part, that nothing could be better done, for the interior of the chapels containing the idols consists of curious imagery, wrought in stone, with plaster ceilings, and wood-work carved in relief, and painted with figures of monsters and other objects. All these towers are the burial places of the nobles, and every chapel in them is dedicated to a particular idol, to which they pay their devotions.

Three halls are in this grand temple, which contain the principal idols; these are of wonderful extent and height, and admirable workmanship, adorned with figures sculptured in stone and wood; leading from the halls are chapels with very small doors, to which the light is not admitted, nor are any persons except the priests, and not all of them. In these chapels are the images of idols, although, as I have before said, many of them are also found on the outside; the principal ones, in which the people have greatest faith and confidence, I precipitated from their pedestals, and cast them down the steps of the temple, purifying the chapels in which they had stood, as they were all polluted with human blood, shed ill the sacrifices. In the place of these I put images of Our Lady and the Saints, which excited not a little feeling in Moctezuma and the inhabitants, who at first remonstrated, declaring that if my proceedings were known throughout the country, the people would rise against me; for they believed that their idols bestowed on them all temporal good, and if they permitted them to be ill-treated, they would be angry and without their gifts, and by this means the people would be deprived of the fruits of the earth and perish with famine. I answered, through the interpreters, that they were deceived in expecting any favors from idols, the work of their own hands, formed of unclean things; and that they must learn there was but one God, the universal Lord of all, who had created the heavens and earth, and all things else, and had made them and us; that He was without beginning and immortal, and they were bound to adore and believe Him, and no other creature or thing.

I said everything to them I could to divert them from their idolatries, and draw them to a knowledge of God our Lord. Moctezuma replied, the others assenting to what he said, That they had already informed me they were not the aborigines of the country, but that their ancestors had emigrated to it many years ago; and they fully believed that after so long an absence from their native land, they might have fallen into some errors; that I having more recently arrived must know better than themselves what they ought to believe; and that if I would instruct them in these matters, and make them understand the true faith, they would follow my directions, as being for the best.@ Afterwards, Moctezuma and many of the principal citizens remained with me until I had removed the idols, purified the chapels, and placed the images in them, manifesting apparent pleasure; and I forbade them sacrificing human beings to their idols as they had been accustomed to do; because, besides being abhorrent in the sight of God, your sacred Majesty had prohibited it by law, and commanded to put to death whoever should take the life of another. Thus, from that time, they refrained from the practice, and during the whole period of my abode in that city, they were never seen to kill or sacrifice a human being.

The figures of the idols in which these people believe surpass in stature a person of more than ordinary size; some of them are composed of a mass of seeds and leguminous plants, such as are used for food, ground and mixed together, and kneaded with the blood of human hearts taken from the breasts of living persons, from which a paste is formed in a sufficient quantity to form large statues. When these are completed they make them offerings of the hearts of other victims, which they sacrifice to them, and besmear their faces with the blood. For everything they have an idol, consecrated by the use of the nations that in ancient times honored the same gods. Thus they have an idol that they petition for victory in war; another for success in their labors; and so for everything in which they seek or desire prosperity, they have their idols, which they honor and serve.

This noble city contains many fine and magnificent houses; which may be accounted for from the fact, that all the nobility of the country, who are the vassals of Moctezuma, have houses in the city, in which they reside a certain part of the year; and besides, there are numerous wealthy citizens who also possess fine houses. All these persons, in addition to the large and spacious apartments for ordinary purposes, have others, both upper and lower, that contain conservatories of flowers. Along one of these causeways that lead into the city are laid two pipes, constructed of masonry, each of which is two paces in width, and about five feet in height. An abundant supply of excellent water, forming a volume equal in bulk to the human body, is conveyed by one of these pipes, and distributed about the city, where it is used by the inhabitants for drink and other purposes. The other pipe, in the meantime, is kept empty until the former requires to be cleansed, when the water is let into it and continues to be used till the cleaning is finished. As the water is necessarily carried over bridges on account of the salt water crossing its route, reservoirs resembling canals are constructed on the bridges, through which the fresh water is conveyed. These reservoirs are of the breadth of the body of an ox, and of the same length as the bridges. The whole city is thus served with water, which they carry in canoes through all the streets for sale, taking it from the aqueduct in the following manner: the canoes pass under the bridges on which the reservoirs are placed, when men stationed above fill them with water, for which service they are paid. At all the entrances of the city, and in those parts where the canoes are discharged, that is, where the greatest quantity of provisions is brought in, huts are erected, and persons stationed as guards, who receive a certain sum of everything that enters. I know not whether the sovereign receives this duty or the city, as I have not yet been informed; but I believe that it appertains to the sovereign, as in the markets of other provinces a tax is collected for the benefit of the cacique.

In all the markets and public places of this city are seen daily many laborers waiting for some one to hire them. The inhabitants of this city pay a greater regard to style in their mode of dress and politeness of manners than those of the other provinces and cities; since, as the Cacique Moctezuma has his residence in the capital, and all the nobility, his vassals, are in constant habit of meeting there, a general courtesy of demeanor necessarily prevails. But not to be prolix in describing what relates to the affairs of this great city, although it is with difficulty I refrain from proceeding, I will say no more than that the manners of the people, as shown in their intercourse with one another, are marked by as great an attention to the proprieties of life as in Spain, and good order is equally well observed; and considering that they are barbarous people, without the knowledge of God, having no intercourse with civilized nations, these traits of character are worthy of admiration.

In regard to the domestic appointments of Moctezuma, and the wonderful grandeur and state that he maintains, there is so much to be told, that I assure your Highness I know not where to begin my relation, so as to be able to finish any part of it. For, as I have already stated, what can be more wonderful than a barbarous monarch, as he is, should have every object found in his dominions imitated in gold, silver, precious stones, and feathers; the gold and silver being wrought so naturally as not to be surpassed by any smith in the world; the stone work executed with such perfection that it is difficult to conceive what instruments could have been used; and the feather work superior to the finest productions in wax or embroidery. The extent of Moctezuma's dominions has not been ascertained, since to whatever point he despatched his messengers, even two hundred leagues from his capital, his commands were obeyed, although some of his provinces were in the midst of countries with which he was at war. But as nearly as I have been able to learn, his territories are equal in extent to Spain itself, for he sent messengers to the inhabitants of a city called Cumatan (requiring them to become subjects of your Majesty), which is sixty leagues beyond that part of Putunchan watered by the river Grijalva, and two hundred and thirty leagues distant from the great city; and I sent some of our people a distance of one hundred and fifty leagues in the same direction.

All the principle chiefs of these provinces, especially those in the vicinity of the capital, reside, as I have already stated, the greater part of the year in that great city, and all or most of them have their oldest sons in the service of Moctezuma. There are fortified places in all the provinces, garrisoned with his own men, where are also stationed his governors and collectors of the rents and tribute, rendered him by every province; and an account is kept of what each is obliged to pay, as they have characters and figures made on paper that are used for this purpose. Each province renders a tribute of its own peculiar productions, so that the sovereign receives a great variety of articles from different quarters. No prince was ever more feared by his subjects, both in his presence and absence. He possessed out of the city as well as within numerous villas, each of which had its peculiar sources of amusement, and all were constructed in the best possible manner for the use of a great prince and lord. Within the city his palaces were so wonderful that it is hardly possible to describe their beauty and extent; I can only say that in Spain there is nothing equal to them.

There was one palace somewhat inferior to the rest, attached to which was a beautiful garden with balconies extending over it, supported by marble columns, and having a floor formed of jasper elegantly inlaid. There were apartments in this palace sufficient to lodge two princes of the highest rank with their retinues. There were likewise belonging to it ten pools of water, in which were kept the different species of water birds found in this country, of which there is a great variety, all of which are domesticated; for the sea birds there were pools of salt water, and for the river birds, of fresh water. The water is let off at certain times to keep it pure, and is replenished by means of pipes. Each specie of bird is supplied with the food natural to it, which it feeds upon when wild. Thus fish is given to the birds that usually eat it; worms, maize, and the finer seeds, to such as prefer them. And I assure your Highness, that to the birds accustomed to eat fish there is given the enormous quantity of ten arrobas every day, taken in the salt lake. The emperor has three hundred men whose sole employment is to take care of these birds; and there are others whose only business is to attend to the birds that are in bad health.

Over the polls for the birds there are corridors and galleries, to which Moctezuma resorts, and from which he can look out and amuse himself with the sight of them. There is an apartment in the same palace in which are men, women and children, whose faces, bodies, hair, eyebrows, and eyelashes are white from their birth. The emperor has another very beautiful palace, with a large court-yard, paved with handsome flags, in the style of a chess-board. There are also cages, about nine feet in height and six paces square, each of which was half covered with a roof of tiles, and the other half had over it a wooden grate, skillfully made. Every cage contained a bird of prey, of all the species found in Spain, from the kestrel to the eagle, and many unknown there. There was a great number of each kind; and in the covered part of the cages there was a perch, and another on the outside of the grating, the former of which the birds used in the night time, and when it rained; and the other enabled them to enjoy the sun and air. To all these birds fowls were daily given for food, and nothing else. There were in the same palace several large halls on the ground floor, filled with immense cages built of heavy pieces of timber, well put together, in all or most of which were kept lions, tigers, wolves, foxes, and a variety of animals of the cat kind, in great numbers, which were fed also on fowls. The care of these animals and birds was assigned to three hundred men. There was another palace that contained a number of men and women of monstrous size, and also dwarfs, and crooked and ill-formed persons, each of which had their separate apartments. These also had their respective keepers. As to the other remarkable things that the emperor had in his city for his amusement, I can only say that they were numerous and of various kinds.

He was served in the following manner: Every day as soon as it was light, six hundred nobles and men of rank were in attendance at the palace, who either sat, or walked about the halls and galleries, and passed their time in conversation, but without entering the apartment where his person was. The servants and attendants of these nobles remained in the court-yards, of which there were two or three of great extent, and in the adjoining street, which was also very spacious. They all remained in attendance from morning until night; and when his meals were served, the nobles were likewise served with equal profusion, and their servants and secretaries also had their allowance. Daily his larder and wine-cellar were open to all who wished to eat or drink. The meals were served by three or four hundred youths, who brought on an infinite variety of dishes; indeed, whenever he dined or supped, the table was loaded with every kind of flesh, fish, fruits, and vegetables that the country produced. As the climate is cold, they put a chafing-dish with live coals under every plate and dish, to keep them warm. The meals were served in a large hall, in which Moctezuma was accustomed to eat, and the dishes quite filled the room, which was covered with mats and kept very clean. He sat on a small cushion curiously wrought of leather. During the meals there were present, at a little distance from him, five or six elderly caciques, to whom he presented some of the food. And there was constantly in attendance one of the servants, who arranged and handed the dishes, and who received from others whatever was wanted for the supply of the table.

Both at the beginning and end of every meal, they furnished water for the hands; and the napkins used on these occasions were never used a second time; this was the case also with the plates and dishes, which were not brought again, but new ones in place of them; it was the same also with the chafing-dishes. He is also dressed every day in four different suits, entirely new, which he never wears a second time. None of the caciques who enter his palace have their feet covered, and when those for whom he sends enters his presence, they incline their heads and look down, bending their bodies; and when they address him, they do not look him in the face; this arises from excessive modesty and reverence. I am satisfied that it proceeds from respect, since certain caciques reproved the Spaniards for their boldness in addressing me, saying that it showed a want of becoming deference. Whenever Moctezuma appeared in public, which is seldom the case, all those who accompanied him, or whom he accidentally met in the streets, turned away without looking towards him, and others prostrated themselves until he had passed. One of the nobles always preceded him on these occasions, carrying three slender rods erect, which I suppose was to give notice of the approach of his person. And when they descended from the litters, he took one of them in his hand, and held it until he reached the place where he was going. So many and various were the ceremonies and customs observed by those in the service of Moctezuma, that more space than I can spare would be required for the details, as well as a better memory than I have to recollect them; since no sultan or other infidel lord, of whom any knowledge now exists; ever had so much ceremonial in his court.

Bibliography

Beezley, William, and Michael C. Meyer. *The Oxford History of Mexico.* Oxford: Oxford University Press, 2010.

Díaz del Castillo, Bernal. *True and Full Account of the Conquest of Mexico and New Spain.* Trans. James Lockhart. Gutenberg Project Ebook.

Elliott, J.H. *The Old World and the New.* Cambridge: Cambridge University Press, 1992.

Pastor, Beatriz. *The Armature of Conquest: Spanish Accounts of the Discovery of America 1492-1589.* Stanford: Stanford University Press, 1992.

Restall, Matthew. *Seven Myths of the Spanish Conquest.* Oxford: Oxford University Press, 2004.

Made in the USA
Coppell, TX
20 April 2022